I0813367

THE HARRY STYLES EFFECT

For the almighty girls we were and the almighty women we are.

And for Liam Payne. Stay made of lightning.

THE HARRY STYLES EFFECT

KERIS FOX

AN IMPRINT OF PEN & SWORD BOOKS LTD.
YORKSHIRE – PHILADELPHIA

First published in Great Britain in 2025 by
PEN AND SWORD WHITE OWL
An imprint of
Pen & Sword Books Ltd
Yorkshire – Philadelphia

ISBN 978 1 39903 083 0

A CIP catalogue record for this book is available from the British Library.

Typeset in Times New Roman 12/16 by
SJmagic DESIGN SERVICES, India.
Printed and bound in the UK by CPI Group (UK) Ltd, Croydon, CR0 4YY.

The Publisher's authorised representative in the EU for product safety is Authorised Rep Compliance Ltd., Ground Floor, 71 Lower Baggot Street, Dublin D02 P593, Ireland.
www.arccompliance.com

For a complete list of Pen & Sword titles please contact

PEN & SWORD BOOKS LIMITED
George House, Units 12 & 13, Beevor Street, Off Pontefract Road,
Barnsley, South Yorkshire, S71 1HN, England
E-mail: enquiries@pen-and-sword.co.uk
Website: www.pen-and-sword.co.uk

or

PEN AND SWORD BOOKS
1950 Lawrence Rd, Havertown, PA 19083, USA
E-mail: uspen-and-sword@casematepublishers.com
Website: www.penandswordbooks.com

Contents

Introduction

> 'The Harry Styles effect is one of self-love and a little naughtiness. But most importantly, it's about putting love into the world and seeing it multiply.'
>
> Dr Louie Dean Valencia

How much do you love Harry Styles? Do your friends send you Harry gifts through the post? Actually, not even your friends, but people you sometimes chat with online who then slide into your DMs saying, 'This is a bit weird, but I saw something and thought of you, can I have your address?' And more often than not the thing they saw and thought of you is that weird little Harry bobble-head doll.

Or do postcards just appear, lots of them, one after the other, from Australia. Harry on the front, nothing on the back. You ask a couple of Australian friends if they've sent you anything and when they say no, you are puzzled. But then you remember an online friend you met once years ago asking for your address for 'something silly'. And the silly thing turns out to be a series of Harry postcards with no context from the other side of the world.

Do you have a Harry doll? Did you buy it in a charity shop for £2 even though it's not wearing any trousers? Does it live on the window ledge in your bedroom next to the Niall doll an online friend sent after it was reduced to four quid in the shop she works in. (She messaged you about it as a joke. You bought it anyway.)

Do you have a One Direction towel that a friend brought over from Australia when a group of you met up for brunch and you all cried laughing at how terrible it is. (You collectively decided it was probably possessed and somehow you drew the short straw and ended up taking it home. It's under your bed. That's probably not a great place to keep a potentially demonic towel.)

Do you always get something Harry-related for your birthday or Christmas? Even though you are 52 years old?

I mean, if you're reading this you probably do, don't you. As someone once tweeted, you have to come to terms that Harry Styles is an actual lifestyle. Either you're all in or you're out. I'm all in. Clearly.

It's fascinating to me how being a fan of someone can feel both entirely personal and totally collective at the same time. We feel like it's just us even though we know for certain it's not. (But do you secretly think it is a bit different for you? You do, don't you. Even when you know full well it's not, it can't be.)

And I could be wrong, but I think it might be worse (or better) for fans of Harry Styles. As Brittany Spanos wrote in *Rolling Stone* in August 2022, Harry is 'someone who is inexplicably difficult to casually enjoy'.

So how did I get into this predicament? In 2014, I was supposedly working on edits of my third novel, but instead I was procrastinating online. I watched a Vine (remember Vine?) of Harry with One Direction on stage in Florida for *The Today Show*.

In the clip, Harry is performing, one arm in the air, but then glances over and makes eye-contact with the person filming. He turns and dances towards the camera. He looks cheeky and knowing. He's being goofy rather than sexy, pretending to be moving in slow motion, but it's sexy all the same. *This better not awaken anything in me*, I thought in a gif of Dean Pelton from Community, because by then I was a person who thought in gifs and had no idea how much worse it was about to get.

And it did. It wasn't sexual (but also it wasn't *not* sexual) but it was a whole world I'd almost forgotten. Or if not forgotten, at least thought it was no longer appropriate to have or to even want.

But on that day in Starbucks, I posted the Vine in a tweet and asked if publishers were still looking for books inspired by Harry Styles, because the six second video I couldn't stop watching suggested I could write a good one. Only took me another nine years.

Since then, Harry's star has risen higher and higher and my fandom has grown stronger and stronger. Falling for Harry Styles has had a positive impact on my friendships, my finances, my sexuality and more.

Fandom, for me, has always been an interest, a distraction and then an obsession. I've rarely liked anything 'a normal amount' as Joey lies about Hugsy, his penguin pal in *Friends*.

When I first fell in love with One Direction (I almost deleted 'fell in love with' because please, but that's how it feels, deal with it), I used to joke it was part of a midlife crisis. Could be worse, eh? This is how my midlife crisis has manifested, I would say. I'm cool with it.

But why does it have to be a crisis, midlife or otherwise? And why do I need to make excuses for it? Joke about it? Can't I just say here's a thing that brings me joy? More than joy.

Early in the film version of the Take That jukebox musical *Greatest Days*, the character of Rachel (played by Lara McDonnell as a teen and Aisling Bea as an adult) is dealing with a difficult home life and finding comfort in her boyband (Take That, but also not Take That).

They're there when she makes dinner for her little brother and sweeps up the plate her dad smashed while rowing with her mum; they're in the bathroom (on the other side of the curtain) while she showers; they accompany her and her friends to school. She calls to them when she needs them. Even though we see them on screen, we know they didn't really come, they're in her head, but the support, comfort and distraction is clearly as real to Rachel as if they are actually there.

(I remember walking to school, shy and nervous, and holding my own curled thumb, pretending it was Andrew Ridgeley from Wham! holding my hand. (I have never told anyone that before.))

Later, Rachel, now all grown up and having won tickets to see the band's reunion tour in Athens, is in her car and leaving a message for her boyfriend to tell him she doesn't think she will go on the trip after all, when she looks in the rear-view mirror and there, crammed into the back seat, singing, are her boys.

'So you're all back then,' she says, deadpan.

It made me laugh out loud.

It wasn't quite the same for me – my (various) boys didn't come back; instead, it was a new band entirely – but the emotions were instantly recognisable. In his book *Talking to Girls About Duran Duran*, Rob Sheffield writes that an adult woman often has 'a slightly mocking, slightly ironic' relationship to their teen music loves, 'and yet she can still feel that love in a non-ironic way'. He goes on to say, 'And when adult women talk about them, they turn into *those girls* again.' *Greatest Days* captures this perfectly.

Towards the end of the film, after the four adult women have had a row in Athens, their younger versions appear next to each of them singing the Take That song, *Back for Good*. They finish the song together – the young and grown characters united in their pain and love – and I found myself doing gulping sobs.

I feel so much closer to teen me than the me I think I'm supposed to be at 52. The 'me' society tells me I should be. Watching these girls and women earnestly singing together made me realise that's what Harry Styles, the Harry fandom, has done for me: brought my teen self back to life inside my midlife self and integrated them and, in doing so, helped me, as Erica Jong writes in *Fear of Flying*, to discover that I was still whole after so many years of being half of something.

My 14-year-old son tells me I have a 'Harry Styles smile'. He says he can tell when I'm looking at Harry on my phone because I get this dopey/dreamy look on my face I don't have at any other time. He does an excellent impression of it.

At Harry's Paris show in 2023, I held up my phone to film the stage and accidentally took a photo of myself, 'Harry Styles smile' in full effect. I laughed out loud when I saw it. I posted it on Instagram with the caption: 'Find someone who looks at you like I look at Harry Styles.'

In the nineties, I worked for the famously miserable music legend, Van Morrison. In two years, I don't think I ever saw him smile. In 2019, a photo emerged of Harry Styles and Van the Man backstage at a show. Harry is smiling at the camera; Van is beaming at Harry. My tweet about this went mildly viral and many of the replies called Van's reaction *The Harry Styles Effect*.

So, what is the Harry Styles Effect?

It's charisma – some might call it the X factor – but it's not just charisma … It's his style and his smile and his hair and his warmth and humour. It's his self-belief and talent and confidence. It is, as Ross says about one of Monica's boyfriends in *Friends*, 'the way he makes me feel about myself'.

In the run up to the release of the 2022 album *Harry's House*, a promotional You Are Home Twitter account posted cryptic pictures and messages, giving the fans clues about the forthcoming album. One of them said simply, 'Dance louder'.

That's what Harry Styles inspires me to do. To dance louder in every aspect of my life.

That's the Harry Styles Effect.

Preface

Lights Up

I should state right up front that I don't know Harry Styles. I've never met him. Everything I think or feel I know about him is based on Harry Styles the celebrity.

As cultural critic Ellis Cashmore writes in the latest edition of his 2006 book *Celebrity Culture*, when we talk about celebrities, we're not actually talking about people; we're talking about how we imagine them.

'In a sense,' he writes, 'they have an existence separate from the physical, living being with human emotions and frailties'.

In her book about fandom and morality, *Monsters: A Fan's Dilemma*, Claire Dederer writes that it's standard practice for an artist like Harry to maintain as much mystery as possible in a world where his every move is dissected to death. 'Indeed, what mystery he possesses comes from our knowledge of the wondrous fact that there's an actual person, a soul, hidden somewhere in the midst of all this information.'

The mystery, even within the avalanche of knowledge, is very much part of why he's as successful as he is.

As my friend Amy put it:

> He very much feels like a blank slate meant to be projected upon, rather than him organically projecting anything outwards. He's almost this kaleidoscopic figure – whatever is shone on him, whether that's fan opinions or stage lights, he bounces that straight back out

> ten times brighter. I kind of like that. This contradictory persona of complete anonymity while being everything and anything his audience needs of him.

It's a tricky balance, I think. And one he manages well most of the time.

At pretty much every one of his shows, Harry gives basically the same speech. It goes along the lines of 'My job for the next 90 minutes is to entertain you. But your job is to have the time of your life. To be whoever you want to be in this room. To love whoever you want to love in this room.'

I have, as of this writing, had the best time of my life at seventeen Harry shows. From Manchester to New York to LA to Australia. I've been to shows alone. I've been with friends I've had for years. And I've been with friends that I met through Harry Styles (including the aforementioned Amy).

I'd be lying if I said I didn't see this coming. I've always fallen hard for boybands, and I definitely have form for not being satisfied with just one show – I literally got a job as a steward at Wembley so I could see New Kids on the Block multiple times – but there's something different about a Harry Styles show.

In 2017, on the way back from seeing him in Glasgow, I sat on the train feeling … something. I wasn't sure what. It was a bit like homesickness? Post-holiday blues? But not quite. I couldn't put my finger on it. And then I saw a tweet that said 'Getting over a Harry Styles concert is THE WORST. I felt like we spent a long passionate night together and he's left me without leaving his number.'

That's exactly it. As one of the friends I went to Australia with puts it, 'there's a real sense of intimacy and belonging where there's often a wall between performer and fan'. This intimacy matters and is present even in a stadium. (Intimate enough that, after dodging it for two years, I caught Covid at a Harry show.)

And the belonging is integral too. Since the One Direction days, fans have taken Pride flags to shows and thrown them on stage. Harry sometimes picked them up back then, but now he does so every show, often during his updated and ecstatic version of *What Makes You Beautiful*, suggesting, perhaps, that whatever each particular flag represents – bi, trans, Black Lives Matter – is, in fact, what makes you beautiful.

In a 2019 interview with *Rolling Stone*, Harry said that, as a white man, he appreciates he doesn't go through the same things as many of the people who go to his shows, he's not trying to say he knows what it's like, he just wants people to feel included and seen. And we do.

At every show, fans ask Harry for advice via signs waved vigorously until he spots them. To a sign asking, 'Should I text him back?' Harry's first response was, 'I have a question: Is he nice to you?'

As someone who spent too many years wondering whether someone liked me and never considering whether I liked them, this was instantly heart-warming. He then went on to say, 'My personal opinion is that if there's any sort of games? Trash, trash, trash, not for you.' Words to live by that also, unfortunately, happen to be a quote from the 2004 movie *The Notebook*. (Harry's love of this dreadful film – and his insistence on calling it a romcom – is, for me, one of the few blots on his copybook.)

Recently, in response to a fan asking for advice after a break-up, Harry told them to fill their own cup and let someone fall in love with the overflow. Which is possibly the best dating advice I've heard in my life and something I think is so deeply important for young women to hear. (Also for me to hear. Might get it tattooed.) He also introduced his song *Boyfriends* with 'To boyfriends everywhere, fuck you!' which I think we can all agree is valid.

'There is something about experiencing the euphoria of an (almost) all-women audience watching something they LOVE,' my friend

Beth says. 'It's unapologetic in its enthusiasm and excitement – there is no jaded, aggressive component.'

Even joining in with shouting 'fuck you' to absent boyfriends is done with more joy than anger. I think it's so important. For young women especially, yes, but also for everyone.

In her relatable memoir of sudden-onset, midlife, celebrity obsession *This Is Not a Book About Benedict Cumberbatch*, Tabitha Carvan writes about how important it is for women to take time for ourselves. She quotes Brigid Schulte calling it 'a courageous – subversive, almost – act of resistance'.

In these, you know, unprecedented times, any act of resistance feels good. And I'd be surprised to find another that feels quite as good as joining a feather-boa-powered *Treat People With Kindness* conga line with glittering strangers.

At one of Harry's 2022 shows, a friend comforted me as I wiped tears away during *Lights Up*. Not a sad song, but a song that I consider to be my pandemic and divorce support song. 'Do you know who you are?' Harry asks over and over. Probably not. Still. But I know myself much better than I did before I fell into the Harry Styles fandom.

I didn't recognise my bisexuality until I was well into my forties. And I didn't accept it solely due to Harry Styles. But the friends I made through his fandom, many of whom have had their own queer realisations, absolutely helped me embrace my new identity. Harry seems to be entirely comfortable in his own skin and it's fascinating to see. He makes me want to be more myself. And the friends I've made through him help with that too. (You'll be hearing a lot about, and from, them throughout this book.)

In 2018, a month after separating from my husband of twenty-two years, I flew to Los Angeles to see Harry finish his second tour at The Forum. I shared a hotel room with fandom friends. I had breakfast with a group of women I'd got to know in a Slack for older (older being over 25; kill me) fans of One Direction. I ordered my first ever Uber to meet two more fan friends for coffee and an American scone (not a scone). And then I had dinner with two women I'd known online through writing Young Adult novels, but who had also fallen for Harry and were seeing him for the first time.

Later, outside The Forum, I drank red wine in a plastic cup as the sun set pink and peach and purple beyond the packed car park our Uber driver had refused to even attempt to enter, and women I'd previously only chatted to online ran up to me, excited to finally meet in person and of course excited to be welcomed, by Harry, to the final show.

I felt, for the first time in a long time, entirely myself. I was far from home in a city I didn't know with women I'd never met before and it felt not only completely right, but satisfyingly healing. I'd lost myself in the later years of my marriage. I found myself again at those shows.

There's an iconic (to the fans) Harry Styles quote about how when he was recording his first album in Jamaica, he ended up drunk and wet from the ocean, toasting everybody and wearing a dress he'd traded with someone's girlfriend. 'I don't remember the toast,' he told *Rolling Stone*, 'but I remember the feeling.'

I remember the feeling that final LA show gave me. That every Harry Styles show has given me. I hope I always will.

Harry Styles and the friends I made through his fandom are now part of the overflow. And Harry is an essential part of how I filled the cup.

Chapter One

The Story of My Life

Are you Ready?

The house lights darken. The stage lights dazzle. Singing the opening lines of the title track of their latest album, my favourite band strides through a swirling cloud of dry ice to appear directly in front of me.

It remains, genuinely, one of the most thrilling moments of my life.

It was 1982 and I had not long turned 11. Bucks Fizz had won The Eurovision Song Contest the previous year with their song *Making Your Mind Up* and my sister and I had fallen in love. (Me with Bobby, my sister with Mike. Both of us with Cheryl – so lovely and pretty and funny. We liked Jay too, but even we could tell she was sexy, so she was a bit scary.)

Our parents had somehow got us – the four of us – front row centre tickets for this show at the Floral Pavilion, our small local theatre. (I've never had such great seats at any show since.) I remember the anticipation. I remember the lights going down and the dry ice – which I'd unsurprisingly never encountered before – filling the stage and pouring over the edge to drift towards us. I can smell it even now (smells a bit like a steam iron).

When my mum was diagnosed with Multiple Sclerosis a couple of years later, I wrote a letter to Bucks Fizz to tell them. I don't think I was expecting them to do anything about it. Maybe I hoped they'd feel so sad for me that they'd come and see me or at least write back. But I think I just wanted to tell someone. I think I just wanted to express that this horrible, frightening thing had happened and maybe they would sympathise. I just wanted to reach out and find someone there who cared.

In the documentary made to accompany the Take That film *Greatest Days*, the film's director, Coky Giedroyc, refers to the band as the main character – Rachel's, 'emotional airbag'. They provide, she says, 'a glorious, gentle cushioning between her and quite a difficult life that she lives'.

I didn't think of Bucks Fizz that way at the time – I think I mostly reverted into the usual fantasies of them turning up at school and taking me away from it all – but I look back now and it makes sense. I was so young. And scared. And confused. And my best friends were always imaginary.

I think about little me when I see the fans at Harry Styles shows with signs about how they've broken a bone or got in a car accident; how it's their first night out since becoming parents, or their boyfriend dumped them for going to the show. So often what's written on the sign has nothing to do with Harry, it's not about music or fame, it's just about something bad that's happened that they want him to acknowledge. And he does. And I hope it makes them feel better.

A while ago, Ava, a writer from London, posted on Twitter/X about how she finds the signs fascinating, so I asked her to explain.

> It's something I think about a lot – where is the line between looking for connection with their fellow concertgoers by creating a moment for everyone to share in, and the genuine exchange between two people, one of them a world-famous pop star and the other a fan?
>
> The thing that fascinates me most about the parasocial relationship between Harry and his fans is that, more than any other I've personally encountered, it seems to go both ways. I'm considering whether parasocial is quite the right word here because this isn't a case of fans taking

interview quotes and projecting them on to their own lives and experiences – they are directly questioning Harry, and he is very publicly responding. It's an unconventional type of conversation, sure, but it is a conversation.

Asking for Harry's involvement in, and advice on, such significant life moments – coming out, gender reveals, and proposals, are all becoming commonplace at shows – feels like a lot of pressure to put on a young man who has had to do all of his own learning and experimentation in the spotlight; who may never have had half the experiences he's trying to give advice on, and definitely doesn't know the nuances involved, nor the specific circumstances of the people asking. In some ways, it wouldn't have surprised me at all if he'd chosen to ignore these signs, and stick to the script, as far as any Harry show has one. But they keep asking because he answers!

The between-song dialogue has, for anyone who considers themselves more than a casual fan, become as much a part of going to Harry's House as the songs themselves. It's a huge reason why I'll personally keep going back – I can't resist knowing what he's going to say next time. I know there must be a line; must be questions he won't answer for whatever reason, be that the pressure of giving the 'right' answer, or simply not wanting millions of people trying to read in to what he's said and relate it back to his life, but he's brilliant at blurring it, and making his audience believe he's absolutely there for them, whatever they need. He makes it seem easy, but it actually feels, to me, pretty brave.

It's brave on the part of the fans, too. These people know the answer they're hoping for, and trust him implicitly to give it, or to come up with something better. To an extent he has to trust them too – to take his answer in the spirit he intended it; not to do anything they don't want to simply because Harry Styles suggested it. 'Are you sure?' he asks a lot, before he helps a fan come out, and in hearing him do so, you realise that while this all feels fun, and like a moment of pure magic, it's a big deal, and it will have gone viral by the time he hits the stage in the next city and probably does it all over again. The fan has to be sure. So does Harry.

♫ ♫ ♫ ♫ ♫

I can't find a source, but I've read a few times over the years that celebrities may become emotionally stuck at the age at which they became famous. I still often think about satirical website *The Onion*'s headline following Michael Jackson's death in 2009: *King of Pop Dead at 12*.

In her 1994 book *Motherless Daughters*, Hope Edelman writes that it's common for women who have lost their mothers to feel stuck in their emotional development 'as if never having matured beyond the age we were when our mothers died'. I suspect this is the case for me, but rather than being when she died, it was when she was diagnosed with MS and everything changed.

A couple of years ago, I was listening to Cariad Lloyd's fantastic *Grief Cast* podcast. She was talking to musician and podcaster Felix White, whose mum died of MS when he was 17. At one point he said that he stopped being a teenager when his mum got ill. I had to stop and remind myself to breathe when he said that. I hadn't thought of it before, but he's absolutely right.

Psychologist Erin Le Clerc says this is common when a parent becomes seriously ill or dies.

'The grief of losing a parent is profound, no matter one's age,' she says. 'Childhood doesn't stop, exactly, but significant grief comes with perspective shifts, changed autonomy, different expectations, so life really can't continue as it had prior to a situation like this.'

Of course, this was the eighties so there was no help, no counselling, not really much in the way of conversation about it even. I remember my mum finding out. I remember her crying about it. I don't remember much else.

I've thought a lot over the years about how I was a rubbish teenager – few friends outside of school, often in a world of my own, happiest alone in my room with music and books – and how I've made up for it since, but I've generally avoided thinking about why that might have been.

A few years ago, I started seeing a counsellor because I knew I should end my marriage but I wasn't brave enough. I think I wanted her to tell me to do it, but (unfortunately) therapy doesn't work like that.

I told her that I'd become obsessed with One Direction and jokingly (but also not really) tried to get her to officially diagnose me with Boyband Distraction Syndrome. Yes, I was probably too old to be so into a boyband, but wasn't that okay? If listening to them, watching their videos, reading about them was making me happy? I told her I'd always had a tendency to get too into bands and did she think that was a problem? She seemed a bit concerned. She didn't exactly say it was unhealthy, but her eyebrows suggested it might be. And she didn't want to talk about One Direction, she wanted to talk about my marriage. Bugger.

Zan Romanoff, one of the YA authors I met first online and then outside The Forum, has written that, for her, being obsessed with One Direction was very clearly a coping mechanism.

'I was barely surviving a depressive episode, Zan wrote for the *Two Bossy Dames* newsletter in 2018. 'I was unhappy or uncertain about work stuff, I hadn't dated anyone I liked in a real way in a long time. Of course I was going to get obsessed with a bunch of cute boys singing about true love.'

Cute boys singing about true love? While my twenty-year marriage was ending? Groundbreaking.

'There's nothing wrong with coping,' Zan says. 'Sometimes that's all you can do! I was dealing with very adult stuff. It was okay to want something to feel simple and joyful and uncomplicated for a couple of hours a week.'

Psychologist Erin Le Clerc agrees. Mostly:

> I think it's okay to seek out fun and distraction as a counterbalance for difficult feelings. However, I think there can be a risk that we lose ourselves in the fantasy of replacing something we've 'lost' and it can become escapist in a way that blocks us from engaging with and solving our troubles for longer-term growth and reward.

I think that was certainly the case for me as a teen, about which more later.

'Dopamine (the "reward" hormone in our brain),' Erin continues, 'is activated when we're doing something pleasurable. The risk lies in seeking the quick thrill (extremely addictive) and can actually sometimes create additional problems on top of the ones we're avoiding. In the end, it's all in the balance. Everything in moderation! Boring, I know.'

Despite my failure to get BDS officially recognised, the main useful thing that came out of my therapy sessions was that I finally realised that my mum's MS and the knock-on effect it had on my parents' relationship changed everything. I've always been a coper. I downplay everything. This is almost certainly where it started.

'I considered the money I was spending on albums and concert tickets and how it wasn't supporting anything particularly noble,' Zan writes. 'But it felt justifiable, somehow, I guess because it felt very clear that it was going to the ultimately noble cause of supporting me.'

I love that. 'The ultimately noble cause of supporting me.'

Because often women don't prioritise ourselves or our interests. And if we do somehow manage to centre something we love, it's so often dismissed as frivolous, not worth the time, effort or expense.

For years, money was a big issue for me. I felt guilty about spending anything at all. I once posted on a money forum looking for advice about this and some man commented along the lines of, 'I don't think you really feel guilty about all spending, do you. You don't feel guilty buying groceries or petrol.' Wrong, random man! I felt guilty about any and all spending, you know, LIKE I JUST SAID I DID.

Part of what fixed my financial mindset – at least partially – was going to America twice in 2018 to see Harry Styles. I went to New York in the June and then when I got back home, booked to go to LA the following month. Ridiculous really. But my marriage had just ended after twenty-two years, I had a bit of money (not enough, a friend paid for my LA flight and I paid her back over the following twelve months), and I just wanted to go and have fun with my friends.

And I did. I had the absolute best time. I sang and danced and ate and drank and laughed and felt more me than I had in forever. In the past, once my bank account was empty, I would fret about every bit of spending. Why did I buy that magazine? I shouldn't have got that coffee. If I hadn't missed that payment then I wouldn't have had to pay a £12 fee. Why was I so irresponsible? Going to America to see Harry (twice!) was probably irresponsible, yes. (And I absolutely appreciate the privileges that allowed me to do it at all.) I don't even know how much it cost, how much I spent, but however much it was, it was also one hundred per cent worth it.

And it finally made me realise that it's almost impossible to put a value on things like that. I could have been sensible, saved the little money I had and stayed home. But I'll always be glad I didn't.

Magical

A couple of years after that first Bucks Fizz concert, I found myself backstage at the same theatre for an annual school show. (I was in the choir but I longed to be a dancer. Unfortunately, much like One

Direction, I was a terrible, terrible one.) Once again, I relished the anticipation and excitement. The smell! Fresh wood and hot dust, and make-up and hairspray.

While I was writing this book, I got in touch with the theatre and asked if I could have a tour. They told me the theatre was entirely rebuilt in 2008 so it wouldn't be the same as I remembered, but I didn't mind. I was interested in the atmosphere, the vibe. The smell.

On the day a nice man named Richard showed me into the theatre and then through to the side of the stage. I definitely got a little frisson of excitement seeing the stage, the lights, the curtain (which was down). He told me everything was bigger than it would have been in the eighties. As I walked across the stage, he raised the curtain (thrilling) and I stood in the centre of the stage and looked out at the empty auditorium.

As I'm writing this now, I'm realising that I should have taken a moment to think about what it would have been like for Bucks Fizz to stand there at the back, waiting. To walk through the dry ice and see the audience. How it would feel with the lights and the heat and the anticipation. It didn't occur to me in the moment though. I was thinking about how I hadn't been able to enjoy being on that stage with the choir because I'd been terrified.

He told me that even though pretty much everything is different, the stage door is in exactly the same position as it was in the old theatre. Until he mentioned it, I'd forgotten about the stage door. Not the Floral Pavilion's stage door, the entire concept of a stage door.

I follow an Instagram account dedicated to photographs of stage doors and every time one pops up it thrills me. They're so exciting. The sense of promise, of glamour and drama. At the Floral, we left the stage, walked down a corridor, peeped at the green room and then we were at the stage door and I realised Richard was showing me out through it. And I was delighted. I'd waited here for Bucks Fizz on the afternoon before the show. I think my dad must have suggested we go and wait in the day because they would be sound-checking and fewer fans would be waiting. He was right.

'I love a stage door,' I told Richard, now.

'They're magic, aren't they,' he agreed.

And then he stepped back into the theatre and closed the door, leaving me outside. I'd expected, hoped for, some sort of epiphany. Or maybe just a connection to little me. I wanted to go back in time, see what she saw, feel what she felt. That didn't happen. I just felt fond. Warm. Happy. I mentally sent her some love.

And then I got my phone out to take a photo of the stage door sign. It was 11:11. Magic.

She Loves You

I was 9 when John Lennon died. I assume I saw it on the front page of the newspaper. I went straight upstairs and woke my mum to tell her, feeling that almost-thrill of being the one to deliver some Very Bad News. My mum, I knew, was a Beatles fan and John was her favourite. And I did that thing people often do when delivering bad news, I giggled. (I felt guilty about that for years, until I had a 9-year-old of my own and realised how very, very young I was.)

(When George Michael died in 2016, I found out on Twitter. I was already in bed and having one last look before sleep. A friend had messaged me with 'I'm so sorry to tell you this …' I actually wailed. So much that my husband ran up the stairs, thinking something had happened to one of the kids.)

This book was already completed when I woke at 3am on 16 October and saw the news of Liam Payne's tragic and untimely death. Rather than attempt to go back to sleep, I went straight to my group chats, where our usual collective joy had turned to collective grief. It still feels almost impossible to think about let alone write about. There should have been so many more chapters in the story of Liam's life.

After her mother died of cancer in 1962, my mum ran away to America to work as a nanny. When The Beatles blew up in '63, she fell for them because they, like her, were from Liverpool and she was young, grieving and homesick. A John Lennon Remco doll stood on our front room window ledge. (Google it. It was hideous. And not dissimilar to the weird little Harry Styles vinyl figures friends kept buying for me because they thought they were funny.)

I'm sure I must have heard The Beatles' music before 1980 – I grew up across the water from Liverpool – but I only started actively listening after Lennon's death. I stuck the front page of *The Daily Star* with its full-page, close-up photo of a young, smiling John and the stark boxed headline 'John Winston Lennon R.I.P. Shot dead by a fan on the streets of New York' on the wall next to my bed, the last thing I'd see before falling asleep, the first on waking. Again, I was 9 years old.

I remember singing *Help* with my friend Angie, who I've known since starting primary school and who remembers my house as being full of music and laughter, which always makes me happy to think about. I vaguely remember Angie and I talking about The Beatles, about John, at school, so I messaged her to ask if she remembered too. Her reply – 'I remember listening to the songs and naming your cushions after them' – made me laugh out loud. I don't remember the cushions.

I do remember that a few years later I had a Paul Young pillowcase. And that in 2017 I saw a One Direction cushion in a charity shop and my eldest said he'd disown me if I bought it. So of course I bought it. I still have it. I hadn't previously realised that I could trace my fandom through soft furnishings.

'I had never heard of The Beatles until you came into class that morning and told me John had been killed,' Angie said.

> Once I learned more and listened more I remember feeling proud that the Beatles were from our town (almost). They showed their movie *Help* on TV that night and that's when I fell in love with them. That movie was definitely going for

> the cute cheeky boyband angle and it had me hooked. They were so cute and funny, the music was fab (pun intended) and the marketing at young girls obviously did its job.

Like me, Angie is still active in fandom. A few years ago, we met for lunch when she was living in the US, but was over in the UK to see Frank Iero, a former member of My Chemical Romance. I'd not long come back from my own trip to the US to see Harry Styles. We compared fandom notes and found a surprising amount in common.

I asked her if she worries about still being a fan in (ugh) middle age? Does she think it's something she should have got over or given up by now?

> Definitely not! I don't think anyone should lose their passions. Why should we give up things that bring us joy just because we got older? And besides, I can afford to buy concert tickets, merch, and albums now. I also support an upcoming band on Patreon and it makes me feel like their invisible, benevolent mother.

Like me, Angie came back to fandom at a tough time, when her son was seriously ill.

> When B became sick, we lost ourselves in the middle of a very dark existence where we were just surviving. I decided to try to find myself again and figure out who I had been before this all started. So I went on my old livejournal and read through all the MCR forums there and I joined tumblr and saw that the fandom was still thriving. It was a lifeline. A connection to what had made me happy in the past and I discovered the spark was still there. I realised what people mean when they say that a band saved their life. Songs have the power to take you

back to a particular time and place, so I effectively used music to time travel back to a happier time and bring the joy back with me to the current time.

Live While We're Young

Back in the early 2010s, I was aware of One Direction – it was almost impossible not to be – but I only really knew their first single, *What Makes You Beautiful*. That one – with its *Summer Lovin'* intro and wildly catchy chorus – had been impossible to avoid.

Once, in a soft play centre when my eldest was about 5 and the youngest a baby, *What Makes You Beautiful* came on and everywhere I looked someone was singing along. The waitress as she weaved between the closely packed tables; a toddler on a trike; a bigger kid on a trampoline; a mum picking at chips one-handed as she breastfed her newborn baby. It's the closest I've ever come to feeling like I was in a musical.

A couple of years earlier, I'd been surprised to see One Direction singing on the back of a lorry at the London Olympics opening ceremony. I googled and was even more surprised to find they were huge and I'd totally missed it. Later that summer, we went on holiday to Mallorca and saw 1D posters in tourist shops. Huh, I thought, they're known outside the UK?

I don't remember how or why, but I know I watched the video for *One Thing*, the platonic ideal of a boyband music video. The five boys – Harry, Louis, Liam, Niall and Zayn, but you knew that, right? – are fresh-faced, adorable, giddy as puppies as they gad about London on a classic open-top red bus, passing both landmarks – Big Ben, St Paul's Cathedral, Waterloo Bridge – and groups of enraptured fans, culminating in ad hoc performances of the song in Trafalgar Square and Covent Garden, while fans and tourists film the band on their phones and the boys pose for selfies.

One of my favourite moments shows fans running alongside the bus, trying to get to wherever the boys would be. And it took me right back.

Madly in Love

My first proper fandom was Bros. Actually I feel guilty saying that because before Bros there was Wham! and before Wham!, Paul Young and Nik Kershaw and Go West, and before them Bucks Fizz. And if you want to go all the way back to see 5-year-old me in a vest onto which my mum had ironed decals of The Bay City Rollers, you absolutely can.

But Bros was different. And I was different.

When they went on a US tour supporting Debbie Gibson, I got the list of dates and venues and wrote them a letter for every stop. I think I was worried that they would be overwhelmed and lonely. Of course, I was the one who was overwhelmed and lonely and desperately looking for connection. But very clearly at a remove. I wasn't going out with – or even attempting to go out with – local boys I actually knew (I didn't know any local boys), instead I was sending letters across the world to boys who had no idea who I was. (And neither did I.)

At 18, I moved from the Wirral to London. I'd been obsessed with the idea of living in London since I was probably about 10 or 11. London seemed to be where everything happened. Where I could become the person I just knew I was destined to be.

It turned out that the person I was destined to be was one who spent almost 5,000 hours (yes, I worked it out) waiting outside Bros singer Matt Goss's Maida Vale apartment block.

Before moving, I'd befriended fellow fans via adverts in the back of *Number One* magazine – it was, in every way, a different time – and one had given me Matt's address. I first went there when I was down in London for the day for job interviews (I didn't have any money or anywhere to live so I'd applied for live-in Mother's Help jobs via the ads in the back of *The Lady* magazine). And I met him, Matt, that very first time. I can still picture him walking towards me (also, I still have the pictures) and feel my excitement, the butterflies in my stomach. I can smell the air (London in Autumn: exhaust fumes and wet leaves). I said hello. He said hello. I asked for a kiss. He kissed me.

It was the most successful interaction I'd ever had with a man. And not just any man – the man whose posters adorned my bedroom walls, whose singing voice could move me to tears. His lips and hands were warm and soft and I was hooked.

From then on, I spent pretty much every minute of my free time waiting for Matt to step outside his home and say hello ("Can I have a kiss?").

A year later, when he at least knew my face, if not my name, we learned that the boys, Bros, were going to be performing at a festival in Paris. Three of us – me, my best friend Sinead and my friend Julie in Liverpool – decided we'd get on a train and a ferry and another train and meet them there. I had my first credit card with a £400 limit and a weekend free from mother's helping. It would be an adventure. I don't remember much about the journey. I do remember being at the airport in Paris, excited to see the boys, giddy at how surprised they'd be to see us. You know, because they usually saw us outside their homes in London and now here we were in an airport! In Paris!

They arrived. They didn't seem all that pleased to see us. They weren't annoyed, they just weren't surprised. I guess if someone waits outside your house for hours on end, you're not going to be that surprised by anything they do. We took some photos with them. We asked them where the show was. Because, of course, this was before the internet. They told us the show was actually at Troyes, a couple of hours south of Paris. And that they would put us on the guest list.

The thought of being on the guest list made up for the fact that we were in Paris and the show was not. We got on a train. (I assume I bought the tickets with My First Barclaycard.) We got to Troyes. We found the festival. Inevitably, we were not on the guest list. Downcast, we joined the French fans that lined the barriers. Eventually, Matt appeared, we somehow got his attention, and he found someone to let us through.

Suddenly we were on the other side of the barriers. Walking to the show with the fans – you know, the losers we'd been just a few minutes earlier – watching us with envy, wondering what we had that they didn't. (What we had was the audacity.) (My memory of this walk of no shame is now superimposed with that meme of the happy little dog who thinks a parade is actually for him. Look at me trotting along! My tail wagging, tongue hanging out.)

We watched the show from the side of the stage. I have a photo of Luke, the drummer, posing at his drumkit, smiling over at me. I have another of Matt, at the front of the stage, one arm punching the air, the crowd blurry in the background. (The photo is from 1991 and not great quality, pretty much all you can see of the crowd is spots of light – which presumably must have been from actual cigarette lighters rather than phone torches – and a couple of raised hands.) Matt's white jeans and jumper are striped with light. The left-hand side of the photo is dominated by the two huge silver spotlights I must have been lurking behind. Like ABBA's Super Troupers. But for once I wasn't somewhere in the crowd, I was on the stage, the lights blinding me.

Night Changes

I saw those One Direction fans in the *One Thing* video and I knew how they felt. The exhilaration of seeing the person you spent all your time thinking about in the flesh, close enough to touch. To smell.

(Fans are always asking what the object of their affection smells like. Even now, thirty-five years later, I remember the cologne Matt Goss wore: Calvin Klein's Obsession for Men.) (On my desk as I write this, there's a 1oz sample bottle of Tom Ford's Tobacco Vanille, Harry Styles' reported cologne of choice that I sometimes sniff for writing motivation.)

It's likely the next One Direction video I watched back in 2014 was *Story of My Life*. It's a more mature song than *One Thing* and the video has a very different vibe. We're shown photos of each of them as children with family members, but each photo updates to the present day. For the family member – as in the song's lyrics – time is frozen: they remain perfectly still while the boys perform the song. Tiny Niall – outfitted in a cricket jumper and playing a violin, his older brother behind him – morphs into adult Niall, who wanders around the room, examining childhood artefacts, his brother trapped in suspended animation.

Liam and Zayn are seen with their sisters. Harry eats cereal on the sofa in a dressing gown while his mum beams indulgently.

And then there's Louis. Infant Louis sits in front of a sofa, a set of doting grandparents on either side. Two of the grandparents age, while the other two fade away. Adult Louis looks back at the empty spaces where his grandparents used to be. And I, who had by then lost all four grandparents and both my parents, who sometimes feels trapped in the suspended animation of those unaddressed traumatic teen years, burst into tears.

It's not hard to see this video as a metaphor for what the five boys lost when they joined One Direction. The childhood and families they left behind. Everyone else standing still while the five of them shot to fame. As Harry's sister Gemma said in an article she wrote for *Another Man* magazine, 'all of our memories became his origin story'.

Fortunately, I'd found my way to the fandom just before their fourth album – cunningly titled *Four* – was released, along with a single:

Night Changes. *Night Changes* is still my favourite One Direction song. Not just because it's a properly great song, but because it makes me so nostalgic. Even at the time it made me nostalgic. When I first wrote this, I wrote 'For what? I don't know.' But then it became howlingly obvious. It's a song about the passage of time, having no regrets, loss of innocence, following your dreams. Truly, I can be dense.

I couldn't stop listening to it. It made me feel the way I felt when I first started listening to music. It made me yearn. And yearning was the predominant theme of my teenage years. (Not long after writing this, I heard the American author and life coach Martha Beck on a podcast. She said we should all pay attention to yearning, it teaches us what we want. 'The only real map of our lives is in our yearning. It is our yearning that takes us forward to what our souls desire.')

My friend Alicia always says that One Direction come to each of us when we most need them and I do think that's true for me. I had a 10-year-old and a 5-year-old. I'd been married for eighteen years. I wasn't unhappy, but I'm not sure I was happy either. I guess I was wondering *is this it*?

And then along came these boys. Apparently living their dream, loving their lives and each other. Travelling around the world and having so much fun. I wanted a piece of it. No matter how small.

As my friend Sophie put it, 'Hearing these young men singing about their delicate, soft and loving feelings cracked open something I must have been guarding in my heart, and out flowed love. Right place, right time, BAM, I was a convert.'

My friend Michael agrees:

> There was something so charming about One Direction from day one, and Harry especially. If I was being philosophical about it, I think we're living through this era where young men in the UK and Ireland have been vilified for such a long time – they're all hoodlums and

> hooligans and ASBOs – but One Direction turned up as this group of incredibly recognisable boys, they felt like lads I knew from school or from work, they felt like lads from my neighbourhood, just sweet and soft and silly, just fun.

I'm not historically a massive fan of straight men. As a group. As a concept. And yet I'm the mother of two sons. I feel a great responsibility to make sure they grow up to be kind and gentle, respectful and loving. One Direction seemed to me like a fine example of healthy, non-toxic, masculinity. They were so physically affectionate. For interviews, they sat pressed together, thighs dangling over thighs, hands playing with one another's hair. It was endearing. They seemed to really love each other and, refreshingly, they weren't afraid to show it. It gave me a smidge of hope.

Spaces

I didn't have long with One Direction before it fell apart. First Zayn left. Like Jay left Bucks Fizz. Like Craig left Bros. Like Robbie left Take That. Like Geri left the Spice Girls. You love a band, you lose a member. The other four carried on and released *Made in the A.M.*, my favourite 1D album. They announced a hiatus (again, not my first rodeo – it's never just a hiatus) and, thanks to friends, I got tickets to see them live.

First in Manchester with a friend who warned me it would be loud. I scoffed. I'd seen George Michael, Bros, New Kids on the Block – I knew loud. As we walked into Manchester Arena, the support act, Jamie Lawson, said he was almost done and then it would be time for One Direction. And the crowd screamed. And I genuinely felt like my head was going to explode, my temples bulged. I had not previously known loud.

We had great seats, right by the stage. At the end of the show, my friend asked if I'd enjoyed it. 'You were just standing there!' she said. I hadn't really known what to do. I'd been transfixed, transported, trying to take it all in. But also I wore high wedge heels because I'm so short and my feet were killing me.

And then it was the last ever show – 31 October in Sheffield. Our seats were at the end of the catwalk and as soon as the boys came on stage and everyone stood up, that was the end of my view. But there was the fan project during *Don't Forget Where You Belong* – signs that said simply 'Home' – that made me sob. There were the friends that cuddled me, laughing, when I cried again all through *Story of My Life*. There was the family conga. The Larry hug. *Act My Age* over and over and over again.

I still can't believe I was lucky enough to be there.

Act My Age

We're constantly told that we're supposed to 'put away childish things' and apparently, for women, that also includes bands or musicians that we love. My parents were obviously on board with my first fandoms – Mum ironed Bay City Rollers stickers onto a vest, they came with us to our first Bucks Fizz shows and then drove us to another, letting us go alone while they, presumably, hung out in the bar.

But by 1988, when Bros kicked in, my dad had been made redundant after his job as a newspaper compositor became obsolete and my mum had been diagnosed with Multiple Sclerosis.

I'm so often still startled at how I can forget the life-shattering impact of those two things, how they changed everything for me as a teen, and how much it influenced the woman I am today.

Chapter Two

Call Me

While I have not yet met Harry, I did once see his mum, Anne, and sister, Gemma, at Euston station. I'd arrived in London to see Harry at Wembley and I'd be lying if I said I didn't wonder if Anne was on my train. I know it passes through what would likely be her closest station. When I got off the train, I saw Gemma waiting beyond the barrier and again I'd be lying if I said I didn't slow down, loiter a little, stop and casually check my phone. And then there was Anne. I watched them hug and then I followed them up the ramp towards the station. I don't mean I followed them in a creepy way, I mean we were all heading in the same direction.

At the top of the ramp, just inside the station concourse, they stopped. And I stopped too. And then I realised – and let me make clear this wasn't a conscious thought, it was more of a feeling – that I don't know them, they don't know me, I have absolutely no association with these people at all. It felt … uncomfortable.

Parasocial relationships are one-sided relationships with people you don't actually know but feel like you do. The concept was introduced by Donald Horton and R. Richard Wohl in 1956, after they'd observed that an increase in media such as radio shows and television had allowed consumers to develop the illusion of a relationship with someone they only knew through media. Which makes me think of those people who knit baby clothes to send to characters in soap operas.

Of course, social media actively encourages the blurring of these lines. We can watch our favourite celebrity's Instagram Stories, get to know their families (know which train station they're likely to use), see what they had for breakfast, how they do their make-up, share their joys and sometimes struggles. And haven't we all been down a rabbit hole of trying to work out the relationship status of a couple of strangers by when and what they last posted about their partner on social media? It's an unprecedented amount of access.

But I often think how odd it must be for famous people when you know them – and know all about them – but they don't know you.

A friend once sat next to a very well-known writer at a dinner party. She'd read all his books and so knew about his wife and his kids, where he lived and why, how he spent his time. With everything she knew about him overflowing in her head, she couldn't think of a single natural thing to talk to him about.

Should you pretend you don't know all the things you know? I used to find it weird when people in real life referenced something I'd said on Twitter, how much weirder is it when strangers know the placement of all your tattoos, have seen how you kiss when you're shitfaced, have read the love notes you wrote to your high school girlfriend?

When I was 19 and living in Richmond, Greater London, I saw the Go West singer Peter Cox on the other side of the street opposite the train station. This was before mobile phones (can you imagine?) and so if ever you approached a celebrity, you asked for an autograph rather than a selfie. I didn't have a pen or paper but I really loved Go West. So I crossed the road, I walked up to Peter Cox, and I said 'I don't have a pen, but if I did, I'd ask for your autograph.' (This sounds extremely confident for teen me, I don't know what I was thinking!)

He was lovely, we chatted a bit, and at some point, somehow, we started walking in the same direction. Together. Still talking. He walked me all the way home. I remember him telling me about working with the very cool music duo Wendy & Lisa, who'd previously worked with Prince. I don't remember much else.

I just looked it up on Google Maps and it is a thirteen-minute walk. Thirteen minutes' exclusive access to someone whose album I had listened to over and over. Someone whose poster I had on my wall. I still can't quite believe it really happened. (It did though, I'm not making it up.) We stopped outside my house. I thanked him for walking me back. I think he said it was nice meeting me. He left. I went into the house and, I can only assume, lay face down on the hallway floor for a while.

Years later, I told someone this story and she said, 'You know why he walked you home though?'

Because he was nice? Because we were having a conversation? Because he enjoyed meeting me?

'No,' she said. 'To stop you following him home and knowing where he lived.'

Oh.

When I started writing this, I joked that I should try to get in touch with Peter Cox and ask him about it, ask him if my cynical friend was right. And then I actually did it. I emailed his management, setting out the above story and asking if there was any chance of a quote from Peter about how that kind of fan interaction felt from his perspective. The following day, I got an email from Peter himself, suggesting we talk on the phone. After checking it was legit and I wasn't being catfished, I replied and we arranged for him to call a couple of days later.

The first time he called, I was on my morning walk, about fifteen minutes from home, pondering popping into Tesco for a pain au chocolat. He said he'd call me back. I spent the remainder of the walk pondering popping back in time to tell my 14-year-old self that one day Peter Cox would call me and I'd say, sorry, now's not a good time.

Back home (I didn't get the pain au chocolat), Peter called again. (It was Valentine's Day. That's not relevant. I'm just saying.)

I wasn't at all surprised (but also, yes, the teensiest bit disappointed) to learn he didn't remember meeting me. But he did say that being approached by fans wasn't something that happened every day, even back then. He said he was probably flattered, but also that he must have had a feeling about me and trusted his instincts. That, for me, is almost as good as being remembered.

We chatted for half an hour about music and the music industry, The Grammys, ageing, Billie Eilish, one hit wonders. He was warm and kind and funny and kept apologising for being boring, even though he wasn't at all. At one point he said something like 'At the risk of boring you with a story I already bored you with thirty-five years ago …' which telescoped me right back to walking up Kew Road, not being able to believe what was happening. (The story wasn't boring.)

Eventually, I told him what my friend said about why he walked me home. Was she right?

'No, of course not.' He seemed offended at the very suggestion. 'I'm not wired that way.'

I believed him. And it just shows, you can rewrite a story. And then rewrite it again.

I've loved the actor Christopher Eccleston since I first saw him in *Shallow Grave* in 1994 (the year Harry Styles was born, oh God). One evening, I was leaving work in Manchester, walking along a sort of passage at the side of the gardens in front of the building I worked in and at the other end of the passage was Christopher Eccleston. I recognised him instantly, I don't know how. (Well, I sort of do, I've done a test and I'm officially a 'super-recogniser' which means I have one hundred per cent facial recognition. But still.)

No one else was around. He was walking towards me. I was walking towards him. I was thinking *oh my god oh my god that's Christopher Eccleston oh my god.* At no point did I consider that he could also see me. Please understand, I didn't think I was invisible. It just hadn't occurred to me that he was a real human person. Until he said "Hiya!" as he passed me. By the time I recovered sufficiently to say hi back, he was most likely back home in front of the TV with his feet up.

In New York in 2005, I saw Paul McCartney on the street. My brain registered that there was a Beatle in front of me. My body stopped dead. I'm pretty sure my mouth dropped open. We made eye contact. I made eye contact with an actual Beatle. And then he went on with his life and I forced my body to start functioning again. From my point of view, that was a sort of thrilling, if extremely weird interaction. And one that must happen to him every single day of his life. What must that be like? How do you live like that?

Obviously, you can't know for sure what you would do until the situation presents itself, but I posted on Instagram asking my friends what they think they would do or say if they ever met Harry. Most said they wouldn't approach him. Maybe nod or wave at him. Or yelp. Or even scream. Laura said, 'I'd tell him he's amazing and thank him for the memories and the music.' But my favourite answer was Amy's: 'Because my first and only encounter was ridiculous, I now have a letter that I carry in my wallet.'

One friend said, 'I think I'd want a hug, but I'd actually ask for a selfie because that would seem more normal.'

I would want a selfie because I would want proof that it really happened. Not for other people necessarily, but for myself. I occasionally spend some time near where Harry lives in London and the fear of bumping into him means I can never even go to the local shop without a bra or make-up (if I ever do meet him, I insist on having visible eyebrows).

A couple of my friends have met Harry. One lives not far from him and saw him running near Hampstead Heath. She said hello, thanked him for his music and told him how he helped her realise she is queer. He asked her name, shook her hand (she said his hands were very soft) and that was it. A lovely interaction.

Another was in a cafe working on her dissertation when she looked up and saw him through the window. She went outside and said hello. She didn't tell him the dissertation she was working on was about him.

While I was writing this book a friend asked me if I idolise Harry. At first I thought of course I don't idolise him! God. I'm a grown woman! And then I thought … maybe that's exactly what I do. So I googled the definition:

> verb: idolise
> admire, revere, or love greatly or excessively.

Yeah, I'm pretty sure I do that. Although I would argue with 'excessively'. Who decides how much love is too much love?

Turns out there's a test for that. In 2002, in response to the growing interest and media coverage of celebrities and their private lives, researcher Lynn McCutcheon and colleagues proposed the concept of celebrity worship and the Celebrity Attitude Scale to measure it. They suggested that while it was normal for children and adolescents to become intensely interested in celebrities and to use them as role models, this 'celebrity worship' should decrease with age.

(I keep hearing and reading that this should decrease with age, but I've yet to see any explanation of why that should be. Also it only really seems to apply to women. Men aren't expected to give up their interests post-puberty. In fact, a man having, say, a lifelong sport fandom is seen as something to be celebrated, to brag about.)

Anyway, these researchers claimed that celebrity worship could become dysfunctional and even, in the most extreme cases, pathological. Unsurprisingly, this theory has been criticised for pathologizing fans and I have to say, just the idea of it rubbed me up the wrong way. I keep googling and reading the Scale, but for a while I couldn't bring myself to complete it. Because I don't really care. Maybe it would tell me I'm unhealthily obsessed with Harry Styles, maybe it wouldn't. What difference does it make? Harry Styles brings me joy. And if all of this stems from a coping mechanism I needed in childhood and never gave up … so what?

(Although I do keep thinking of it as the Celebrity Attachment Scale after attachment theory, which is the idea that the way you bonded with your earliest caregivers sets the foundation for how you approach relationships for the rest of your life. Perhaps my insecure attachment to my parents led to an over-reliance on imaginary relationships with celebrities. Discuss.)

But I'm inherently nosy, so eventually I gave in. I couldn't figure out the scoring, but reading the statements, it's easy to tell which are considered 'borderline pathological'. Yes, I like to talk about Harry Styles with my friends. No, I don't believe Harry and I have our own secret code so we can communicate through the TV or radio. And, yes, I do think he'd be upset if he found me sitting in his car.

'It would be great if my favourite celebrity and I were locked in a room for a few days' gave me pause. I mean, yeah. Who hasn't thought about that? I wouldn't lock him in a room against his will, but if we both somehow got trapped in, say, an Ikea (there's one near his mum's) for twenty-four hours, I'm not going to complain about it.

As I wrote this book, I kept thinking *this is too much about me*. I mentioned this to a friend who said, wisely, 'fandom is only ever vaguely about the fan-subject'.

I thought about that as I listened to a podcast in which comedians and writers Sara Pascoe and Cariad Lloyd discussed Esther Yi's novel *Y/N*, about a woman obsessed with a member of a K-pop band.

As a teen, Sara Pascoe was a huge Take That fan. I've heard her talk before about how she daydreamed about the band's car breaking down and how they'd have to come into her house and eat beans on toast. Ordinary things. On the podcast, she talked about waiting outside the TV show *The Big Breakfast* when Robbie Williams was presenting.

Sara remembers staring at the back of Robbie's head, focusing intently, willing him to turn round and look at her. But she didn't want him to talk to her or even really see her. She didn't feel seen, didn't want to feel seen. She felt ugly and like she didn't really exist.

She says, 'the idea of Robbie Williams seeing the outline of me … I thought "I will start existing when he notices me"'.

This stopped me in my tracks.

I don't think I ever felt like I would start exiting when he noticed me, but I suspect I used to think that Matt Goss noticing me would bestow something on me. If he liked me, it meant I was likeable. If I made him laugh, I was funny. I showed him the drawing I did of him and hoped he would tell me I was talented. I wanted his approval and validation.

As Tabitha Carvan writes, 'It's no longer just to do with a celebrity … it's about how you see yourself in the world.'

Waiting outside Matt Goss's flat, alone in London aged 18, I didn't know who I was. I look at the photo I took of myself in Paris – yes, I'm looking at Harry Styles, but I'm not wanting or expecting him to look back – and it feels like me.

Chapter Three

Falling

I almost always dream about celebrities and have done for as long as I can remember. Sometimes a dream leads to a crush. It happened with Paul Weller in my teens, David Mitchell (comedian not author) when I was pregnant with my first child (I watched so many of his TV shows that my unborn baby used to respond to his voice, as if he was the actual father). And then, in 2014, Harry Styles. It wasn't a sexy dream, but I tweeted about it, as I used to tweet about pretty much everything, and a friend responded with a Harry gif.

I don't know if you spend much time online, but there is a Harry Styles gif for pretty much every occasion and emotion. I searched for a gif with which to respond. She replied with another and by the end of the day we were talking about One Direction and she'd given me a list of videos and interviews to watch. I was 43 years old. A full-grown adult woman. I'd been married for eighteen years. I had two children. I wasn't really in a boyband place. And yet.

There was something about One Direction.

Can I just pause here and mention that it's increasingly possible to talk about Harry Styles – to be a massive fan of Harry Styles – without reference to One Direction. But not for me. I loved 1D first and I still consider myself a fan of the band and of the individual members (to differing degrees). Yes, Harry was my favourite from the start, but, for me, there's no Harry Styles without One Direction.

Which makes it increasingly baffling to me when I see Harry fans who became fans during his solo career. It makes perfect sense and

God knows, I have no right or intent to gatekeep, but it makes me feel both old and astonished. I saw a TikTok of someone who'd just seen the Met Gala promo clip of Harry eating popcorn while wearing 3D glasses. The caption said 'im struggling with this ive never seen it?!?' and the comments were filled with equally astonished fans asking where it was from.

I simply cannot imagine being a Harry fan who hasn't hung on his every word for the past 10+ years. A friend once texted me that she was on the same flight as him. I replied, 'Is he wearing a stripy jumper?' Her response: 'Keris. What the fuck?' I'd seen photos of him at the airport on an update account.

I didn't go to the Met Gala in 2019, but I did go to New York to watch the Met Gala on TV with fan friends. A bunch of us stayed in an Airbnb in Brooklyn and more friends joined us to watch the event on TV. We waited with bated breath and much drink and many snacks for his outfit reveal. We watched and cheered and laughed and cried and danced and cuddled. I indulged in my first and last weed gummy. It reminded me of the gas and air I huffed during labour with my first child. It made me feel like I was in slow motion. It made me anxious and jittery. It made me beat a constant path between the kitchen sink (for water in) and the bathroom (water out). I apparently cannot even be drugged into losing control (again, more on this later).

My One Direction fandom didn't end when the band did, partly because I'd become so close to my fandom friends. It was the same with Bros. We came for the band, sure, but we stayed for the friends. And in 2016, it was different because of the internet. Whereas in 1989, I had to phone my friends, often from a phone box (fans would call the phone box near Matt's house and any fans nearby would answer. 'Has he come out yet?' 'No, not yet, but his car's there.'), by the time I fell for One Direction, I was already Extremely Online.

First, my new fandom friends and I talked on Twitter, and then joined the Slack for older fans. And then we branched out from there to the group chats that are still my first port of call when I pick up my phone in the morning.

Before long, the boys started releasing solo music. I first heard *Sign of the Times* when Nick Grimshaw played it on his Radio One breakfast show. I was standing in my kitchen, the radio on, already typing in the group chat as we waited to hear just what Harry was going to do outside of the band.

I still have the messages:

Keris: I'M LISTENING RIGHT NOW
[07/04/2017, 08:04:59] Keris: (On radio 1)
[07/04/2017, 08:06:30] Keris: jesus
[07/04/2017, 08:06:35] Keris: I love
[07/04/2017, 08:07:14] Jenni: So excited!
[07/04/2017, 08:07:57] Lindsay: Oh my God. He sounds amazing
[07/04/2017, 08:08:08] Georgie: literally got to my internet as the song finished fml
[07/04/2017, 08:08:12] Keris: IMAGINE IT LIVE OMG
[07/04/2017, 08:16:19] Georgie: i'm dead
[07/04/2017, 08:16:19] Georgie: on the floor
[07/04/2017, 08:16:20] Georgie: d
[07/04/2017, 08:16:20] Georgie: e
[07/04/2017, 08:16:22] Georgie: a
[07/04/2017, 08:16:23] Georgie: d
[07/04/2017, 08:16:43] Keris: Right? RIGHT?

Reading that back still makes me laugh. The anticipation. The excitement. And we had no idea what was coming next.

A tour was announced, and I got tickets for Manchester, the Apollo, the same venue as my first Bros concert in 1988. A friend came up from London and another two friends including Georgie (d e a d in the above group chat and who I'd known online since she tweeted me about one of my books) who flew over from Australia.

'My best friend and I had a fair amount of disposable income and time to travel, and so we decided we would go to England to see his first solo "home" show in Manchester,' Georgie told me. 'Looking back now, it was amazing to be able to see him in such a small venue! I captioned my pics from that night "the closest I have ever come to a religious experience", and that really sums it up.'

Inside the venue, we stood near the back, by the bar, but before long, I wanted to get closer. One benefit of being a much older fan is that people will assume you're someone's mum and not stop you casually wandering right down to the front of the stage. Once there, I didn't really know what to do apart from take a couple of photos (and think *wow, look, he's right there*). And then, despite my advanced age, a security guard told me I couldn't stay at the front. I hadn't been planning to anyway, the fans on the barrier had queued and likely even camped out to claim their position, I wouldn't push in. I just wanted to be there. Right there. To look up, see Harry on the stage, and think, yep, he's real.

I appreciate this sounds ridiculous coming from a woman in her forties (as I was then), but one thing fandom has really brought home to me is that I don't feel any different to the me I was the first time I saw a show in that same venue, aged 17, wearing snow-washed black jeans (with green stitching) and yelling myself hoarse when Matt Goss dropped his Levis to reveal Union Flag boxer shorts. (Actually, one difference is that I don't really yell. I sing along. I might whoop. I'll almost certainly cry. But yelling and screaming is not my thing – more about this later.)

As a teen and into my twenties, I was never satisfied with just seeing an artist I loved once, and it turned out that nothing had changed. Along with Georgie, I saw Harry again in a small venue in Glasgow and then, when an arena tour was announced for the following year, in London, Birmingham, Manchester and Glasgow again.

I once read a tweet in which someone said they were trying to explain to their therapist how seeing Harry live changed the way they saw the world. (I completely identify with this.) The therapist said, 'What you're describing is presence. He's fully present, in the moment.' Seeing Harry live reminds me of watching the International Space Station fly over. It reminds me of how big the world is. How many opportunities and ways to be there are. It makes me want to do more, live more and better.

The Australian author Simmone Howell wrote a brilliant piece about how we're all created by everything we've read and watched and dreamed about. (I would add 'listened to'.) In the piece, she quotes the tagline for the movie *International Velvet*: 'In every girl is the woman she is destined to become … And in every woman is the girl she used to be', and I feel that so strongly in relation to music obsessions.

I've seen Harry live seventeen times. I've seen Barry Manilow live ten times. The two of them played Manchester on consecutive nights in 2023 and I was gutted that I couldn't manage a Harry/Barry double bill. But the problem with going to see someone you've seen ten times over twenty-something years is you can see all the previous versions of yourself scrolling out behind you.

I've never seen Barry Manilow without thinking of the first time I saw him at the Royal Albert Hall. I was 20 and I went alone and bought my ticket outside on the night (the only time I've ever done so, and I was sure it was going to be a sting and I'd be immediately arrested).

About ten years ago, I saw George Michael live (for the last time, although I didn't know it then). Each song he played took me back. To teen me in my bedroom, yearning, thinking about growing up and leaving home and creating my own life and what that life would be. And as he sang, I thought about how my life was in some ways exactly what I imagined (house, car, husband, two children) but in many ways nothing like I'd dreamed (no bloody money, for one). And of course you can't go back and do it all over again. I cried so much that a stranger further down the row passed me a tissue.

'I'm a video cassette that keeps getting taped over and I get a little shakier with each recording,' as Howell wrote.

I once tweeted that *She Used to be Mine* by Sara Bareilles could take some credit for my divorce and a stranger replied that it could for hers too. "The way it hit me in the gut was the beginning of the end."

Bareilles sings about not recognising herself and thinking about the girl she used to be. I could never get through the line about giving everything back for the chance to start over without crying. I wouldn't do that – I couldn't because I would lose my boys – but, God, I understood the impulse.

Before I properly fell into the One Direction fandom, I read a biography of Harry for research for a YA novel I was writing about a teen celebrity. The biography was published in 2013 (my novel was never finished, let alone published). I don't remember much about the book, but I recorded on Facebook at the time that my then husband had jokingly told me 'to stop going on about Harry Styles so much'.

Four years later, we split up. Did my obsession with Harry Styles cause the end of my marriage? No. But, honestly, it didn't help.

The way Harry lives his life – or appears to live his life – helped me realise that I wasn't living mine, not in the way I wanted to. Of course, I didn't and don't expect to have a life like his – apart from anything else, it looks exhausting – but I knew I needed to be brave and make some changes.

One of the women Tabitha Carvan spoke to described her feelings for Benedict Cumberbatch as 'an affair of the mind'. Someone else didn't tell their husband because they didn't want him to ruin it: 'I didn't want to hear what he'd say.'

For me, it was a bit of both. I wanted something just for me that made me feel like myself again. And that made me realise I hadn't felt like myself for a long time. It made me miss the me I used to be. It made me wonder if I could get her back. (She used to be mine.) And it was just fun to be thinking about Harry Styles all the time!

Like my friend Liz says, a new obsession makes you so happy but you're also distracted all the time and can't think about anything else. 'Like having a massive crush, it feels like new love.'

It felt like a delicious secret and I was into it.

And while maybe my husband wouldn't have ruined it – he did buy me a One Direction mug for Christmas 2014 – it just wasn't something I wanted to share with him.

I asked Martina how her husband feels about her fandom:

> Dave's seen me go through obsessions many times since we first got together twenty-two years ago, so I think he's just kind of used to it now. It hasn't been an issue for him at any stage, I don't think. At least, he hasn't made it evident to me if it has been. I mean, I have never specifically gone on and on about Harry's looks to Dave, but I'm fairly sure he's realised that Harry is attractive and that I may find him attractive. Dave can appreciate him as a musician and likes some of his songs, and if I asked him to, he'd come with me to a concert and probably somewhat enjoy it. I don't think Dave's ever been obsessed with anything in his life, so it's all very foreign to him, but he's never been one to judge or to be disapproving of anything that makes me happy.

My friend Syndea's husband is supportive too:

> He's a generous guy at heart and we may be at the "anything that brings you joy is a good thing" stage of marriage. He finds Harry charming and, as a musician, appreciates that the band is so incredible. That said,

> I have never found him playing any Harry on his own, but he'll let me know if he hears it in the wild.

Psychologist Erin Le Clerc suggests the timing of my Harry obsession wasn't coincidental.

'If you've been unhappy in a relationship, I think when that relationship ends, we have a tendency to try and regain what we've lost. If a sense of adventure, fun, and youth was something you felt you'd lost/wasted, it would make sense to seek out something to fulfil that need.'

In her book, Tabitha Carvan asks what kind of mother becomes obsessed with a celebrity she doesn't even know. I've been trying to think whether I worried about this aspect of my fandom along with all the other things I worried about, but I'm not sure I did.

I've always thought it's important for my sons to see me doing things I love. Things away from them. Maybe things they wouldn't understand (they don't). One thing I did feel slightly guilty about was the money I spent travelling to see Harry at various times, mostly because a couple of times I had to cancel travel plans I'd made with the boys. I explained to them that since arrangements for the Harry shows had been made far in advance, flights and hotels had been booked and often I was sharing accommodation – and therefore expenses – with other people, that those trips had to take priority because I wasn't willing to let my friends down. But, honestly, I wasn't willing to let myself down either. I just don't believe I have to put my own interests aside and prioritise theirs and I don't want them learning this either.

Having said that, when I mentioned to my 14-year-old, Joe, that I wanted to chat with him about my Harry fandom for this book, the first thing he said was that it was a waste of money. He's never mentioned football with his dad being a waste of money. Not even when they got stuck in traffic on the way and missed most of the game.

In her book about Dolly Parton, *I've Had to Think Up a Way to Survive*, Lynn Melnick writes 'Our society expects mothers to prioritise their families or else suffer deserved repercussions.'

She goes on to say that when she allows herself to be the priority and something goes wrong, she feels it as a consequence. It's certainly something I thought about when I went to Australia to see Harry without my boys. Despite most of me thinking that I'll never die (it just doesn't seem like something I would do), there's a tiny part of me that's constantly reminding me I could die at any time. So there was no way I was going to fly to the other side of the world without considering the possibility that I might never come back. And would it be worth it? To see Harry Styles?

'She died,' I imagined people saying. 'All the way over in Australia. And, you know, she went there to see Harry Styles!'

That's not a good enough reason. Work, maybe. A family emergency, of course. But just for fun? I don't think so.

My eldest, also named Harry, but no, not after Harry Styles, thinks it's a good thing that I have something I love and that brings me joy.

'But I don't like Harry Styles,' he insists on telling me.

Harry – my Harry – went to his first proper concert a couple of years ago. Michael Bublé. (I got his dad to take him.) Afterwards, when I asked if he'd enjoyed it, he said 'Now I understand why you go and see Styles so much.'

He regrets saying this now because I bring it up so often.

'I like him,' he says, of Michael Bublé. 'But I wouldn't go to Australia to see him.'

My younger son used to be on board with the whole One Direction/Harry thing. He knew the songs and planned to come with me to see Harry in 2020. I even bought him a pink suit to wear at his request. But of course those shows were cancelled and by the time touring resumed he'd, he says, grown out of it. His music taste changed. He loves the rapper and singer Juice WRLD, who died in 2019. He's watched his documentary over and over. So he understands fandom.

But, he says, the Juice WRLD fandom is different to the Harry Styles one. *Cool*, I expect he means. Not cringe.

Whenever I go away to see Harry (or for any other reason), the boys stay with their dad. Joe, it turns out, sees this as selfish on my part because it inconveniences his dad. I had no idea he thought this. His dad is always happy to spend time with both of them. It's in no way an inconvenience for him to look after them. But, it seems, Joe values his dad's time more than he values mine.

But I don't know why I'm surprised. Society values men's interests more than women's.

In a 2022 Substack essay 'Who Gets "Quality" Leisure?', Anne Helen Petersen examines how the majority of male-dominated/male-coded hobbies take place away from the home and require significant and prolonged time commitments, while female- dominated/female-coded hobbies tend to take place 'within the domestic sphere'. Women's hobbies 'blend with the rhythms of domestic life'.

It's fine for my boys' dad to go to football, or to spend the weekend at a rock festival, and it's fine for me to like Harry Styles, as long as I do it quietly. And preferably at home.

Petersen talks about golf. About how golf is dominated by men. And how for many men, part of the appeal of golf is how much time it takes. It's a hobby that takes the player 'mentally and physically far from the responsibilities of home'.

She wonders if there's any female-dominated hobby that takes as much time away from the home as golf.

I've never played golf, but my dad did. In later years, he played every single morning. I have a cousin who plays a lot of golf and also goes on golfing holidays with his friends. I texted him asking if he ever feels guilty about taking time away from his family, from his responsibilities, for golf. Golf! He didn't reply. Maybe there's no phone reception on the golf course.

Chapter Four

As It Was

There's a 2011 One Direction TV special called *A Year in the Making* that documents the first year of One Direction, from coming in third place on *The X Factor* to releasing their debut album in the UK. There's a moment where Harry is speaking to the camera and says that he was disappointed with his vocals during their first live performance post-*X Factor* – on the Ant & Dec show *Red or Black* – and made the mistake of searching himself on Twitter. In fact, he searched 'Harry shit'. With predictable results. In the documentary, he gets emotional as he talks about the vitriol he unsurprisingly found there.

And then, choking back tears (if you google 'Harry Styles crying' this moment has been widely giffed), he says, 'I've always wanted to be one of those people who didn't really care that much about what people thought about them, but I just don't think I am.'

It's this moment I think about when I see him in a dress on the cover of *Vogue*. When I see him dancing like no one's watching on stage in front of 80,000 fans. When he dropped to his knees after inducting Stevie Nicks into the Rock & Roll Hall of Fame. He seems to me to be someone so entirely comfortable in his skin, so completely cool with who he is, that I genuinely cannot even imagine. And it fascinates me that he got from one state of affairs to the other in just a few short years.

There's a Joanna Lumley quote that I find really inspiring. She says the secret to life is to love everyone you meet. 'From the moment you meet them. Give everyone the benefit of the doubt. Start from a position that they are lovely and that you will love them.'

I don't know for sure that this is how Harry lives his life, but I would be surprised if it's not. And it's how I'd love to live mine, but I don't think I do. Certainly not with men (with good reason) but I would like to try to be more open, more vulnerable, to risk being let down rather than not allow anyone to get close in the first place.

In an interview for *TIME* magazine, the actress Jennifer Coolidge talks about how Harry puts it all on stage, 'There's self love and love of the world and love of other people. It's such an attractive thing. I was thinking how confident he was and I was like "Why didn't it occur to me to be like that?"'

It didn't occur to me to be like that either. I think because it can be embarrassing to be seen trying. To be (or appear to be) your authentic self. Wholeheartedly. It's what I want for myself. It's what I feel like I've been working towards – with varying degrees of success – my entire life.

So to see Harry go from a 16-year-old vomiting with pre-stage nerves, googling himself with the sole intention of reading horrible things people said about him, to someone who exudes confidence, who seems entirely comfortable in his own skin, is inspiring to me.

One lesson that I did learn a long time ago, is the ability to laugh at yourself. As Nora Ephron put it, 'When you slip on a banana peel, people laugh at you. But when you tell people you slipped on a banana peel, it's your laugh.' A big part of writing for me (and the internet has been a major contributor to this) is telling people about my banana peels. Sometimes, literally as something bad or embarrassing is happening I am already composing messages about it in my head.

These days, Harry seems to be comfortable with making mistakes, with fucking up and failing. Following the technical issues at the Grammys (honestly inexcusable, but not his fault) he said on the final

James Corden show that at first he was angry, but then 'I thought — the only thing that's gonna happen is, I'm gonna shout at someone and it'll still be the same and then they'll think I'm a dick.'

Many stars (including, allegedly, James Corden) are more than happy for people to think they are dicks. And many people wouldn't stop to consider the potential outcome before losing their shit over something like that. The fact that Harry did – and chose not to flip out – suggests a level of poise to which I suspect most of us can only aspire.

After the *Don't Worry Darling* press tour debacle resulted in Harry being accused of spitting on Chris Pine – something I couldn't and still can't believe people thought was a thing that genuinely happened – Harry joked about it on stage at Madison Square Garden, telling the crowd, 'I just popped over to Venice to spit on Chris Pine.'

Harry always gets the joke and doesn't even seem to mind when he's the butt of it.

It's a wildly attractive and, for me, inspiring quality.

Because while I am now adept at getting my own banana peel laugh, I can still be quite a baby when it comes to people laughing at me.

It can still feel embarrassing to be seen. Writing this book has been such a joy, but every now and then my stomach lurches – like when you drive too fast over a hill – and I realise people are going to read it. You're just putting it all out there, eh? I ask myself. Apparently I am. Oh God.

I am always trying to be more Harry.

I'm sure if you're reading this you already know Harry's origin story, but here's a quick summary. He was born in Redditch, grew up in Holmes Chapel. His parents divorced when Harry was 7 and his mum, Anne, remarried first a man named John Cox (the family lived above a pub) and then Robin Twist, who sadly died of cancer in 2017.

It was Anne who sent in Harry's *X Factor* application and Anne who listened to him practice (from inside the bathroom because he was embarrassed for people to look at him when he was singing). Anne is also ever-present during the *X Factor* journey, by Harry's side as he's interviewed in the queue outside Wembley, backstage hugging Dermot O'Leary after Harry's successful audition. Also present is Harry's older sister, Gemma, whose life was also irrevocably changed once her baby brother was launched to fame.

In an article for *Another Man* magazine (released with three different Harry covers; full sets are currently listed for around £3,000 on eBay) Gemma wrote about how the family accompanied him to the first *X Factor* audition. They didn't expect or, of course, want him to fail, but nor did they expect that 16-year-old Harry was about to be launched into international superstardom. Who would?

One Direction were a young band and Harry was the youngest, just 16 when he went to the audition and never returned home. The band spent five years riding a ridiculous wave of fame, travelling around the world, dealing with rumours, press intrusion, fan obsession, everything that comes with being a wildly successful boyband.

From the start – truly, the start, search One Direction first auditions on YouTube if you're not sure – Harry was the one who most epitomised the X factor. The other four are various combinations of charming, talented, funny, cheeky, sweet. Harry has it all, along with an absolute boatload of charisma and, evidently, self-belief.

So when One Direction announced their hiatus in late 2015, it was Harry that everyone assumed would 'do a Timberlake'. (Thanks to Britney's memoir, the meaning of this is forever changed. Fo'shiz.) Although I don't think anyone genuinely expected him to be as successful as Justin Timberlake, or even to eclipse the achievements of the band that spawned him.

In a 2017 Apple Music documentary (that I have watched at least a dozen times), Harry says he's come to terms with the fact that his solo career is unlikely to be as successful as the band. But by the end of 2023, not only was his latest tour, Love On Tour, his highest grossing solo tour (and the fourth $600M tour ever), it also out-grossed One Direction's entire touring career.

Some credit obviously must go to Harry's management – Jeffrey Azoff, son of music management giant (in reputation if not in stature) Irving Azoff, who has not only managed The Eagles for more than thirty years, but has also been an agent, concert promoter, film producer, record label owner and CEO, and music publisher. Harry chose them knowing exactly what they could do for him. To call it a smart move would be a massive understatement. As my friend Dawn put it, 'You don't get to where he is by accident.'

Unlike many bands, One Direction never seemed to have a problem with having a majority female fanbase and Harry has continued and expanded that, giving the impression that he both relishes in and respects the fans he has. He's not waiting for a male audience to bestow credibility or legitimacy. He knows what the fans have given and continue to give and he appreciates it. And he just flat out seems to love and respect women, which is as appealing as it is rare.

Tabitha Carvan says that by never criticising One Direction, allowing the fans to keep the memories of the band intact, Harry set the scene for how those same fans then embraced him as a solo artist.

'We can trust that he's not going to turn around and say actually, that wasn't me, that was embarrassing,' Tabitha says. 'You don't have to erase that part of yourself.'

In performing One Direction songs on stage, in transforming *What Makes You Beautiful*, Harry is saying that was me then and you were there too. I'd love you to come along with me now.

I watch these old videos now when Harry was 16, 17, 18, 19, 20 and I look at my own sons – one 15, the other 20 – and I can't imagine it at all. How does it feel to be the mother of a 16-year-old who not only left home for an audition and never came back, but was then thrust into international fame and everything that comes with it?

In One Direction's 2013 documentary *This Is Us*, Harry's mum talks about how she feels like she should be the one showing him the world, instead she's in New York to see him perform at Madison Square Garden. Liam's mum keeps a cardboard cut-out of him in his bedroom because she misses him so much. Zayn's mum is overwhelmed with gratitude for the house he – at 20 years old – has bought for his family back in Bradford. 'I can't even thank you enough for what you've done for us,' she tells him, crying.

I cried too when I watched it. It's too much. Their relationship forever changed. The dynamic flipped.

Robbie Williams was also 16 when he joined Take That and he makes it pretty clear in his 2023 Netflix documentary that it resulted in enormous and ongoing trauma. Yes, he says he was predisposed to mental illness anyway, but he also points out repeatedly that fame is toxic. I thought about Robbie's mum while I watched. Robbie's mum whose name I know (Jan). Who I can picture (along with his dad, Pete) because I was obsessed with Robbie.

In the early nineties, I worked for iconic journalist and TV presenter Paula Yates, and so when Take That presented *The Big Breakfast*, I went along. I chatted to Robbie in the green room and thought he was adorable and hilarious (and, unusually for a celebrity, much taller than I expected). He asked if I wanted to hang out in the make-up room while he and Gary Barlow got ready. Of course I did.

I remember standing just inside the door, not sure what I should do, but thrilled to be there. There were so many fans outside, but I was inside. Properly inside. I could not have been more inside! The only fan in the make-up room.

And then someone told me I had to leave. Gary had apparently asked them to tell me to leave. Typical Gary.

Robbie had made me feel special. Gary put me back in my place. Yeah, I had extra access, but I was still just a fan.

I get it now though. Maybe, for Gary, the make-up room was one space where he didn't have to think about fans, he could just relax and be himself. God knows, the more famous you get, the fewer of those spaces are available.

I love how open Robbie has always been about fame. I loved his books with Chris Heath, *Feel* and *Reveal*. *Feel* includes the best analogy for being massively famous I've ever heard and I tell people about it all the time. I can't quote the book, so I'll paraphrase it (from memory, so apologies if I've misremembered or embellished).

Imagine you're out one day and someone throws a ball at you. A light one, it doesn't hurt, but it makes you look and go 'Oh!' And then the next day, there's another. And then there's a few. And then it's relentless. Every time you leave the house, people are throwing these little balls and some hit you and some miss and even on the rare occasions no one's throwing them, you're bracing yourself because there could be another one at any time. How would you ever relax? And I don't think Robbie says this, but while most of the balls are light and harmless, surely every now and then – and the more famous you are, the more often this must happen – some of the balls are bigger and heavier and absolutely will hurt.

I once read the actor Josh Hutcherson recounting that being approached by fans isn't the worst part; the worst part, for him, is when he sees that someone has seen him and he can tell they're trying to get up the courage to approach him and he can't concentrate on what he's doing because he knows he's probably going to be interrupted at any time.

There have been stories recently of Harry approaching fans. Perhaps he does it because he wants to talk to them, to make a connection, but perhaps he's just heading them off, so he doesn't have to wait, he can get on with his day. Of course, the two aren't mutually exclusive. Proactively approaching fans doesn't mean he's not interested in a connection. Years ago, I heard a story about a famously miserable rock star being approached by a fan in a cafe. As the timid fan arrived at the side of the rock star's table, the rock star snarled 'Fuck off' without even looking up from his soup. (The fan fucked off.)

Harry's third album, *Harry's House*, debuted at No.1 in the UK and stayed there for six weeks. In the US, it had the largest sales week of any album that year. The first single, *As It Was*, was No.1 for ten weeks in the UK and US and hit the top of the charts in another thirty-three countries. Love On Tour included fifteen-date residencies in both New York and Los Angeles.

When unveiling the fifteen nights banner at Madison Square Garden, American TV personality (and, yes, Oprah's best friend) Gayle King called Harry 'walking joy, walking happiness, walking love'.

During an interview with Zane Lowe in 2019, Harry compared preparing for success with surfing, saying that you can practice getting up on the board, but sometimes the wave doesn't come. At other times, the wave comes, but you haven't practiced getting up on the board enough and you're not ready for it. 'Every now and again,' he said, 'you've practiced enough and the wave comes … I kind of always wanted to be prepared to get on the board when the wave comes.'

Harry was ready. And the world, it seemed, was ready for him.

Chapter Five

Sign of the Times

After hearing a rumour that Matt Goss from my beloved (at the time) Bros was dating Radio 1 DJ Jackie Brambles (she went by Jakki back then; ah, the nineties) my best friend and I came up with a plan to go and check her out. As far as I can remember, we rang Radio 1, said we were interested in working in radio (or maybe we said we were writing an article about working in radio) and could Jackie give us any advice. She invited us down to BBC Broadcasting House. I can remember sitting chatting with her in a hallway outside the studio. She was friendly and encouraging and afterwards we felt pretty guilty for having tricked her into the meeting.

When I think back on this, I wonder why I never thought about a career in radio. I loved radio. I used to get my mum to record my favourite show, *Steve Wright in the Afternoon*, while I was at school, reminding her to turn the ninety-minute cassette over after forty-five minutes. I can still sing some of the jingles. The only time I ever bunked off school was to go to enter a competition on Simon Bates's show to win tickets to the Wham! Final concert, and to go to the Radio One Roadshow in nearby Southport. (Despite my painful shyness, I volunteered for Bits & Pieces, a quiz where you had to guess a song from a snippet. I was chosen. I went up on the stage. I won. I got carried off stage by Gaylord the Gorilla, which was actually comedian Phil Cornwell in a gorilla suit. This remains one of the greatest achievements of my life and if I ever tell anyone around my age, they are always wildly impressed.)

I suspect I was never able to imagine anything that wasn't 'the talent' and because I knew that I didn't have the confidence (or indeed the talent) to be a DJ or a singer or musician, I ruled the whole thing out.

In *Girls Just Want to Have Fun*, their analysis of Beatlemania, Barbara Ehrenreich, Elizabeth Hess and Gloria Jacobs conclude, 'If girls could not be, or ever hope to be, superstars and madcap adventurers themselves, they could at least idolise the men who were.'

Did idolising (mostly) men from such an early age stop me from doing something for myself? Is that why I was never ready to get up on the wave?

'I think often teenage girls are positioned to be observers/supportive/fans of men because that's what women do all the time in life,' says Dr Carrie Dunn, who wrote her doctoral thesis on female football fandom and has since written a number of books about women's football. 'So rather than *doing,* they channel energies into this obsessive fandom.'

This resonates with me. Uncomfortably so. I recently read *This Is What It Sounds Like* by Susan Rogers and Ogi Ogas. Rogers writes about loving music but having no talent for performing. She remembers seeing a photograph of an engineer at a mixing desk and realising there were ways to work in music that didn't require her to be a musician. I find it so odd that I never had a similar epiphany.

I daydreamed about being a musician, despite having no musical talent.

I tried writing songs. I both adored and was wildly envious of Debbie Gibson (she follows me on Instagram now – when I got the notification, I made a sound like a monkey blowing a vuvuzela) who was just a year older than me and who had released her debut album *Out of the Blue* at age 16, having written all the songs herself.

I wrote two. One was called *Skyline*, and while I remember six lines of it (there may have only been six lines of it) they are mortifying and I will not be putting them here. But I remember two lines of another song called *Wild Horses* 'So if you're choosing to stay, wild horses couldn't drag me away', which I still think is quite good? But I remember looking at them, thinking that a) they weren't good enough and b) I wouldn't know what to do with them anyway, and that was the end of that.

After moving to London, I wrote to every record company and music publisher in the Yellow Pages, but I was offering myself up for admin jobs. (I'd learned to touch type at night school while working as a mother's help. Every word of that sentence makes me feel ancient.) Why didn't I think of training to do something else? Partly, I think, it's about class. I was told more than once as a teenager that people like me didn't do things like that. When I met with the school careers officer, I told her I wanted to be a photographer. With an air of wanting to catch me out, she immediately asked what camera I used. I was nervous and couldn't remember. She suggested, condescendingly, that if I didn't even know what camera I used, I should hardly think I could be a photographer. And I believed her.

I talked myself out of everything that scared me.

But what if I hadn't? What if I'd channelled my fandom into something for me? When I told people I was writing this book, so many of them said something like 'Your whole life has been leading up to this!' I said it myself. And as I've written it, I've made so many connections, spotted so many patterns that hadn't occurred to me before.

But also while I was writing this book, my youngest and I watched the Tina Fey sitcom *30 Rock*. In one scene, Liz Lemon tells her producer, Pete, that he needs to slash the show's budget. Proudly, he says, 'My whole life has been building to this moment,' and then he cringes in realisation: 'Oh God, has it really?'

I wrote fanfiction before it was even called fanfiction. I wrote self-insert stories about George Michael and Andrew Ridgeley fighting over me. About travelling the world with Duran Duran and Spandau Ballet (who probably fought over me). I put myself in films and music videos. I was in Switzerland for the *Last Christmas* video, falling off my skis adorably before flirting with both Andrew and George over a candlelight meal back at the lodge. I wrote constantly, feverishly. (Before I moved away from home, I just as feverishly scribbled over every page of those books, before wrapping them in Sellotape and pushing them down deep into the outside bin.)

After I moved to London, my friends would commission me (unpaid – that should have been an early lesson) to write romantic and sexy stories featuring them and their faves in fantasy situations. They told me I was good at it. It still took me about ten years to think maybe I could be a writer and another ten to actually do it. (And a further ten to get published.)

One of the things that blew me away when I first fell into the One Direction fandom was the abundant creativity expressed by the fans. An absolutely startling amount of fanfiction, yes (search One Direction on Archive of Our Own, a non-profit, open-source, repository for fanfiction and other fan works contributed by users, and you'll get over 78,000 results), some of it beautifully written and more entertaining than many published novels, but not just fanfiction.

Sacha Judd, who I got to know through the 1D Slack and who, in 2022, became movie website Letterboxd's Senior Harry Styles Correspondent, speaks at conferences on various subjects including how fans will transform the world. In a talk she gave at Beyond Tellerrand in May 2022, she said she realised she'd been spending so much time trying to think about how to engage women with technology, while ignoring the fact that they already were:

> They were essentially already video editors, graphic designers, community managers. They were teaching each other CSS to make their Tumblr themes look more gorgeous, and they were using Chrome extensions in

> anger to make Tumblr do what they wanted. These were basically front-end developers, social media managers, they were absolutely immersed in technology, every day, and we weren't paying attention, because they were doing it in service of something we don't care about.

One of the things that surprised and delighted me when I joined the Slack was how many of the women were working in fandom-related jobs and industries. For film studios and in TV. For Wattpad and celebrity social media. In theatre and comedy. And there were so many writers. All doing exactly what they want to do in the industries they love.

Sam Fong, another friend from the Slack, works for TikTok and I asked her if her job came out of her fandom.

> The TikTok algorithm knew I was a big One Direction fan and it kept serving me content during the pandemic at a time when it was scary and I was unemployed and it made me want to work for TikTok even more. I never searched for any 1D or Harry content. They just knew.

This made me laugh because I have so many women friends around my age who were suddenly served an abundance of Harry content via TikTok with predictable results. I've had so many DMs from friends who have suddenly found themselves overwhelmed with Harry feelings and know that I will understand.

I don't know when the TikTok algorithm first served me one of Dan Cash's videos, but he soon became one of my favourite creators. He started making TikTok content about One Direction in 2021 and now boasts over 350,000 followers of his entertaining, relatable, and often hilarious videos. His most popular Harry video with over a million views features Dan's suggestions of who he wanted to see perform with Harry at Coachella. (His nomination of Elton John made me realise that's probably not going to happen now, which makes me sad.)

'I started with silly videos about their song lyrics, highlighting all the innuendos and the things that didn't really make sense,' Dan told me when I asked him how he began.

> And then that took off, with my videos getting millions of views, so I started sharing my love for them as soloists. I also did similar style videos about their solo songs. By the time Harry started the second leg of Love On Tour, he seemed to have just grown in popularity so quickly. My videos grew and grew, and it was amazing to share my love of his music with so many people across the world. I always try to keep my content light and funny, as well as insightful and sometimes educational. There's so much to talk about when you've been a fan of somebody for over ten years, and it's been incredible to share it with so many people.

College student Lexy Jones runs her own small business inspired by Harry and his music. Her bright retro designs featuring lyrics and quotes paired with cute graphic illustrations are immediately eye-catching. I asked her how it came about.

'I was bored during the first quarantine back in 2020,' Lexy told me, 'so I spent hours making designs and I posted them on my Instagram every day.'

At first, Lexy sold via Redbubble (who manufacture and ship everything) and then Etsy, which meant she started making and shipping everything herself.

'I sold stickers, jewellery, keychains, prints, and more. I did this for about two years and made a decent amount of money, but more importantly just had so much fun creating everything, doing my own product photography, and making and shipping everything from my dorm room.'

After Etsy cracked down on fan art for copyright reasons, Lexy started creating her own site.

'I'm waiting until I graduate and get settled to start up again so that I can offer even more products like apparel. But for now, I'm just posting the designs on Instagram and having fun doing that.'

And all of this came out of being a Harry fan. 'Posting art for all the world to see is a very vulnerable thing,' Lexy says,

> and not only is the art inspired by Harry's lyrics, his vulnerability in releasing the music also inspired me to show the world my art in the first place. It has been the most rewarding thing I have ever done. It has given me purpose and a supportive community to be my most authentic self.

Chloe also has a business selling Harry related prints and stickers. She too started an Etsy after having a few Instagram posts that hit thousands of likes and progressed to stickers and custom orders for prints and some clothing. After Etsy shut down the fan shops Chloe, like Lexy, set up her own website.

'I do love having a shop and being able to bring a little bit of joy to people with the things I sell. I am hyper critical of myself and anything I create. But I always hear Harry saying, "don't worry about it, everything's going to be just fine".'

Quilter, Liz Harvatine – a good fandom friend, although we've yet to meet in person -was also creatively inspired by Harry:

> A few months into my Harry obsession, I started a quilt intended to be hung in a quilt show. It's not an exaggeration to say most of my waking thoughts revolved around Harry, so of course he became my design inspiration. This was 2018, fresh after the end of touring for HS1, and the current image the world had of Harry was suits and

> flowers and sparkles, all rolled up in a beautifully tailored package. The quilt incorporated techniques and design elements that I had been exploring pre-Harry, rendered using wool suiting, large scale floral prints, gold lamé, and metallic quilt ties. It felt like a pure influence of Harry's 'being' on my artistic expression. One of the greatest comments I received about the quilt was from someone who didn't know its name or inspiration. She said it was a perfect blend of masculine and feminine, which I then realised was exactly what I loved about Harry's style. He has a sort of androgyny in which he's not genderless but rather combines elements from more extreme ends of the spectrum. A perfect blend of masculine and feminine.

That blend of masculine and feminine also inspired one of the most unhinged – but also most fun – expressions of my fandom. It started when a friend described Harry's Victoria's Secret fashion show look – a mint green Givenchy suit – as 'a delectable macaron'. For some reason – I was almost certainly procrastinating on a deadline – I googled mint green macarons.

'Is there already a Harry as macarons Twitter?' I posted, referencing the abundance of accounts comparing/matching Harry with inanimate objects including breakfast foods, book covers, art, dogs, the sky.

A friend shot back, 'I can't find one so someone is obligated to start it now.'

And I, despite being 46 years old, thought … okay.

For the next three years – yes, three years – I looked for a macaron to match pretty much everything Harry ever wore. Sometimes, I would see an outfit and think there was no way I could find a macaron to match. And then I did. He was photographed with a Shiba Inu (Bell, maybe you follow her on Instagram) and I found Shiba Inu macarons. He posed with a harp for *Saturday Night Live*, I found a harp macaron WITH STRINGS (I actually added a note to this one saying yes it is indeed a macaron; I didn't think anyone would believe it otherwise).

I found neon macarons, tie-dye macarons, Mickey Mouse macarons. Glitter, smiley faces, lace, tattoos, flamingos, pumpkins, Pokémon.

I even found penis-shaped macarons for when Harry wore a Keith Haring Safe Sex T-shirt. He once wore a Chicago Cubs T-shirt and pink trousers combo that matched the macarons I found so perfectly that I started to wonder if he'd seen the account and was challenging me. (CHALLENGE ACCEPTED.)

'How am I going to macaron that?' is something that I, an adult woman, with two kids and a job, thought on a regular basis.

But do you know what? It gave me a massive sense of achievement. I realised that I was really good at colour and pattern-matching. I kept thinking that I have a good eye for this kind of thing. What kind of thing? Matching macarons to photos of Harry Styles? If only that was a transferable skill. And then it kind of was. Because when Covid hit, I started painting.

Of course I began with paintings inspired by Harry's music. Eventually I did a painting for every song on all three albums. I sold most of them but kept a few for myself. I found that I loved waiting for the music to suggest themes and patterns, combining the colours and waiting for the little click of rightness when I knew a painting was done.

I hadn't really done any art since school. I'd loved it then and was fascinated by the idea of art school, but, again, didn't think it was for someone like me. One of the few pieces I remember doing for A level was a pencil portrait of George Michael in the *Wake Me Up Before You Go Go* video. Body twisted at the waist, his elbow is pulled in at his torso, head bowed, hands curled into fists between finger clicks. The light and shade of the creases and folds of his T-shirt, the distortion of the words Choose Life. It took forever. I loved it.

Later, I drew Bros. Matt and Luke. I was so proud of it. I showed it to my dad, who loved to draw, saying 'The noses could be a bit better …' He replied, 'They couldn't be much worse.' For years, I couldn't tell that story without crying. Eventually I had a session of EFT Tapping (Emotional Freedom Techniques) specifically to take the sting out of that particular memory and how I felt it had affected me creatively. It worked. (Also, I got the drawing signed by Matt and Luke. They both admired it and didn't seem to have a problem with their noses.)

Again, until I wrote this, I hadn't considered how the Harry art I did during lockdown connected me with teen me. I feel like she's been trying to reassert herself all this time and I kept pushing her back down. I'm glad I finally listened for long enough to let her out.

In 2012, I was both writing young adult novels and articles for teen magazines. In a copy of *Teen Vogue* I bought for research, I spotted a photo of a boy carrying two Starbucks trays – eight drinks – and laughing, his dimple popping, his hair a luxuriant Lady Di sweep. *That*, I thought, *is a YA love interest*. I tore the page out and added it to my research file.

Clearly, I wasn't the only one. Harry specifically, and One Direction generally, are mentioned so often in novels now that I started the Instagram hashtag #putonedirectioninallthethings which, over the last few years has mostly been Harry in all the things (I feel guilty even writing that; sorry to the other boys, I will try to mention you in my books) (look, you're in this one!).

Friends look out for it now and message me to tell me they've found another book for me to add to my 'to be read' pile, but honestly it's getting to the point now where I'm surprised if Harry's not mentioned in a book I'm reading (even cookbooks – Harry Styles's Dutch Baby with Cinnamon Rhubarb in Ruby Tandoh's *Flavour*). Or a TV show I'm watching. Or a podcast I'm listening to. He gets everywhere. (I took a break from writing this to watch an episode of Richard Osman's *House of Games* and one of the questions was about Harry. Plus, I knew it was about Harry before the question was even asked 'This person had a Saturday job in a bakery …')

When Harry started popping up in books written by many of my author friends, I suspected they were doing it on purpose to sneakily check if I was reading their stuff. (A couple of them have admitted this is indeed the case. Or if not to check up on me, to make me smile. Totally works.)

My author and screenwriter friend Cat Clarke took it one step further (and is therefore my favourite) by putting *me* in her middle grade novel, *The Pants Project*: 'There was nothing about her to suggest she was a crazed One Direction superfan. She had curly hair, cool glasses and a friendly smile.'

It me! (But I'm not crazed. I'm just excited.)

When asked on the *Weirdos Book Club* podcast why the main character of her book, *Really Good, Actually*, fantasises about Harry, Monica Heisey said, 'We needed a sexy, rock star person, but a lot of sexy rock star people seem like they would be bad boyfriends.' In contrast, co-host Cariad Lloyd suggests, you feel like Harry would protect the heartbroken woman at the centre of the book. (This is indeed very much part of his appeal.)

The other host, Sara Pascoe, pointed out how busy Harry must be in fantasies, which both made me laugh and is also another good example of Ellis Cashmore's assertion that a celebrity has 'an existence separate from the physical, living being'. There's the real Harry, Harry Styles the popstar, and then the infinite fantasy Harrys who exist only in our fevered imaginations.

Harry also appears as a fantasy figure in Sarra Manning's novel, *The Man of Her Dreams*.

'He's one of several fantasy boyfriends of the heroine and much mention is made of "shit tattoos",' Sarra told me. (I bristled, ridiculously, at every mention of the shit tattoos when I read the book. Some of them are shit, certainly, but not all of them!) 'I feel like he's a fantasy figure for a lot of women, especially those with a liberal sensibility,' Sarra continues, unaware of my tattoo-based offense, 'and it was also a nice little in joke for my friends who were very amused by my crush on Harry, which started in lockdown.'

I've known Sarra online for years – I did my first ever author event with her and was so intimidated, but she was lovely. She used to tease me about my Harry feelings, so I was delighted when she finally fell for Harry too. But *The Man of Her Dreams* wasn't the first time Sarra had based a character on Harry:

> I used him as the inspiration for Louis in *The Worst Girlfriend In The World*. The lead singer of a quite appalling local band in a little seaside town, who became the object of lust for the two main female protagonists. I characterised Louis/Harry as being 'young, dumb and full of cum', but also a quite benign presence. One of those beautiful boys that seem quite intimidating but that's all projection and when you get to know them, they're just a delightful idiot. I feel now like maybe I maligned poor Harry back then.

One of my own characters fantasises about Harry in my adult romance *It Had to be You* – she works in a bookshop and daydreams about him coming in one day. And the pop star in my novel *My Heart Goes Bang* is entirely Harry-inspired. (I really struggled to come up with a name as good as Harry Styles, which is just a properly great pop star name, right? I eventually went with Dylan Jewell. It's good, but it's not Harry Styles good.)

In her wonderful 2018 YA novel about fangirls, *Ship It*, Britta Lundin has a secondary character named Caty 'who is free-wheeling, fun-loving, and dresses audaciously, and every single one of her outfits is a riff on something Harry has worn.' A floral blazer, a bow tie, a flamingo-patterned shirt (that flamingo shirt is one of my favourites from Harry's extensive patterned shirt collection).

I've done this too. In my novel *One Italian Summer*, the love interest, Luke, who wasn't based on Harry, but who everyone assumed was because he has long hair, wears one of Harry's casual fits.

'He's wearing long black shorts and a white T-shirt with bright lime-green trainers,' my main character says. 'He's got sunglasses on top of his head. I want to lick his neck.'

They do say write what you know.

I can't write about fantasy depictions of Harry Styles without mentioning *The Idea of You* by Robinne Lee. First published in 2017, Lee's novel became a massive pandemic hit and was later made into a film starring Anne Hathaway and Nicholas Galitzine. While Lee says that the book wasn't inspired by Harry – it clearly was, come on – *Grazia* magazine described the film as being based on 'Harry Styles fanfiction'. *Vogue*, however, called the plot a 'socio-cultural commentary about ageing and a woman's worth'.

There's no reason it can't be both.

The cover of Bebe Ashley's first poetry collection, *Gold Light Shining*, is distinctly Harry-inspired, featuring an illustration of the white high-waisted trousers with double row of gold buttons, in the pose Harry is striking on the cover of his second album, *Fine Line.* I asked Bebe how the book came about. Like so many fans I spoke to, she fell down the One Direction rabbit hole thanks to the YouTube algorithm.

'Harry's vocabulary and consideration of what he was saying caught my attention,' she told me:

> I started researching One Direction and was shocked at the immense pressure they were put under and the constant scrutiny from the media. So I wrote my first 'Harry' poem only using words and phrases he'd said at some point in interviews as a critique on how he had to trust other people to represent him.

Seeing Harry live in Birmingham in April 2018 (I was also at that show) confirmed for Bebe that he was something she wanted to write about:

> I'd turn up to my writing workshop and people would ask if this was another Harry poem, which I would often refuse to confirm or deny. All these connections to Harry Styles started popping up in my life so I just kept writing poems that explored some of those. For example, I visited Jordan on a cultural exchange and one of our cultural partners complimented my Harry T-shirt and suddenly we were off talking about Harry. I got a travel scholarship from my university to visit Camp: Notes on Fashion at The Met, so when I got back, I wrote a couple of poems. I never expected to end up with a book but as I kept enjoying the work, I kept writing and I've never once regretted it.
>
> I'm now writing the most personal poems I've ever written and I don't think I'd be able to write these if I hadn't written all the Harry poems first. At first people would laugh a bit when I said it was a book inspired by Harry but I've had some incredible opportunities since writing that book that I never would've experienced if I hadn't started writing, and then kept going. I've been on the radio, I've been on TV, I've done readings. I'm scared of all of those things but I did it anyway!

Lucy James, 21, from Wales, wrote her university dissertation about the Harry fandom. She was studying theology and religion when the idea came to her at one of his Wembley shows in 2023. Her dissertation is titled, 'Are Fandoms Comparable to Religious Groups?: The Harry Styles Fandom a Case Study'.

I spotted Lucy's story online and was intrigued since it's something I've wondered about too. I'm not religious, but standing in a crowd looking up at a man, it's hard not to see parallels. In her dissertation, Lucy suggests that the love and devotion fans have for Harry is expressed in a similar way to that of established organised religion. The dissertation looks at fandom pilgrimages, community and ritual. It's not only an interesting and entertaining read, but it also introduced me to the concept of 'collective effervescence', which comes from Emile Durkheim's *The Elementary Forms of Religious Life* and is defined as 'the feeling of energy and harmony when people are engaged in a shared purpose'.

It feels to me like the perfect encapsulation of the vibe of a Harry show.

And Lucy is not the only one to address Harry academically, Dr Louie Dean Valencia, Associate Professor of Digital History in the Department of History at Texas State University, created an entire Harry college course. I emailed him to ask, basically, why (and also can he run it online so that I can take it). He told me:

> As a historian and researcher, I usually spend my summers doing research in Europe. However, during the summer of 2020, because of the pandemic, like most people, I was homebound. Through the early pandemic and into the summer, Harry's music became a lifeline and a comfort for me. As someone who studies youth culture and the ways young people change the world, I started to think more intently about his impact on the world. Over the course of the following year, still teaching classes on Zoom, I found that one of the best ways to connect with students in a world that was all virtual was sharing about music – and Harry's music became a way to connect with those students.
>
> The news of the class made it into hundreds of media outlets globally once I posted about it in the summer of 2022 on Twitter. The first 'volume' of the class filled within minutes – taught in the spring of 2023.

At the time of our emails, he was about to start the latest semester, which he was calling 'Volume II'.

'To be honest, it's the most fun I've ever had in a class and has been really great for students to learn and debate about their contemporary world, but also to learn some very practical skills.'

I asked if anything has come out of the class that he didn't expect.

'I think the media attention was somewhat expected, but not to the level that it was. Mostly, I'd say what I didn't expect was to get so many emails from teenagers to retirees – all wanting to share their love of Harry.'

For some other fans, Harry has provided more than inspiration; he's been life-changing.

Mary, 48, currently pursuing a double Master's in Library and Information Science and Museum Studies at the University of Oklahoma, met her wife through One Direction.

'The four shows of Harry's first tour were basically our honeymoon,' Mary says.

> We got married in Vegas at the beginning of July and then went to follow Harry around California – Sacramento, San Jose, and then both shows at the Forum in Inglewood. We were in the pit in Sacramento and had a sign that said 'We're on our honeymoon and we met because of you', but he didn't read it.

Mary and her wife also have matching Harry tattoos – the words 'Sweet Creature' along with some laurel leaves.

At least two more long-term relationships arose from the Slack. One couple is married, another engaged.

On the topic of tattoos, a friend recently posted an Instagram Reel by Running Water Tattoo in our group chat. The reel asked 'What do you think are the top three most popular Harry songs for tattoos?'

I clicked through and saw that they've done a lot of Harry tattoos and also followed Louis on tour with plans to also follow Niall. Obviously, I slid into their DMs.

Running Water Tattoos is three best friends from Ukraine. Alina and Julia are the tattoo artists and Katie runs the social media and bookings. It was Katie who answered my questions.

> We started kind of by accident. It was Harry's birthday [show] in Palm Springs and an influencer was throwing a themed party. Someone suggested I bring Alina along to tattoo people. We organised the flash sheet of designs in a couple hours and left for Palm Springs the next day.
>
> I was going to follow Louis Tomlinson on tour and Alina, Julia and I thought how cool would it be to do the same thing on his shows as we did for Harry. But none of us were big on TikTok or Instagram. I posted a couple of videos I had from Palm Springs and we went viral and the rest is history.

Their most popular designs are Harry's butterfly tattoo and 'we'll be alright' in Harry's handwriting. Katie herself has the butterfly, a quote from *Keep Driving*, and 'You're so golden' in Harry's handwriting. (I now also want 'You're so golden.')

Alina was already a full-time tattoo artist and Julia does tattoos alongside her main job as a photographer, but this project became a full-time gig for Katie, giving her the opportunity to leave the restaurant industry.

Using Harry as motivation helped Georgie through some mental health challenges.

> I stopped drinking back in 2016, and went to AA meetings for a while, and in AA they want you to have a 'higher

> power'. For a lot of people, that's God or some form of religion, but it can technically be anything that makes you want to be a better person (I may be fudging technical meanings here, but this was my interpretation!). It was initially a joke, but I always said that my higher power was Harry because he would want me to be healthy and the best version of myself. After a while it actually started to help, and I stuck with that way of thinking.
>
> Along the same lines, my friends and I also made a self-improvement group chat called 'Make Harry Proud' where we would share our wins in terms of health, finance, life, or just anything that we said would make Harry proud of us if he knew. [Full disclosure: I am in this group chat.] I haven't had a big brave moment, but he's definitely been there through a lot, and I like to think I'm a better person because of how he inspires me to be.

Amy's daughter Manhattan was born at twenty-six weeks. Twelve inches long and weighing around a pound and a half, with underdeveloped lungs, heart, and grade 3 bleeding on both sides of her brain.

'Manhattan was in the neonatal intensive care unit for six months before she was allowed home,' Amy told me.

> Because of the brain bleed, her official diagnosis is cerebral palsy and autism. The doctors didn't expect her to live at all or any longer than a year or two. She is physically and neurologically delayed and disabled but she's also 17 now with minimal health issues. When you have a child with physical and neurological disabilities, beyond all the medical stuff, you really just want your kid to be happy. Like, over the moon happy. And something that parents of disabled kids have to accept is that, a lot of

the time, you can't provide that happiness and you can't even figure out what can.

Music has always been so incredibly important to Manhattan. Very early on, I realised music is the key to getting her to sit through doctors' appointments and minimise the screaming during physical therapy sessions. When Manhattan discovered One Direction, it was like all the pieces locked into place. She was really drawn to Harry and I ran with it. Anything I needed her to do, I'd find a photo or a video of Harry doing it and it'd be pretty much a done deal. She needs to eat more fruit? Cue Harry eating a banana. Needed her to attempt standing on her own? Bought a Harry cutout and she went straight for him.

She says exactly five people's names and one of those is Harry's. He has inspired her to sing, to attempt speech, and the list goes on and on. As a single parent, I jokingly call him my co-parent and after all these years, it really isn't a joke anymore. There's something about him that reaches a part of her that I could never reach. And maybe she would've found something else but I'm so glad she found Harry.

Chapter Six

Music (is not just for a sushi restaurant)

In her book about fame, former actor Justine Bateman (who I loved in the US sitcom *Family Ties* in the eighties) compares fame to projected love and intimacy, writing, 'I heard your music … I opened myself up to you then, I opened a vulnerable part in myself and I let you in.'

Through their music, Bateman writes, the artist is also vulnerable and so artist and fan meet in that place together. It's one of the best descriptions of the relationship between performer and fan I've ever read.

When I first outlined this book, I didn't even have a chapter about Harry's music. When I realised, I felt embarrassed. As if I'd let him and myself down by omitting the most important thing. But I think it was because I don't think of his music as a *category*. It's the whole point.

When I spoke to Tabitha Carvan, she asked me what was more important to me about Harry, his looks or his music? For a second, I was torn. I immediately pictured his face, his smile, his eyes, his ridiculous arms. But then I thought, if I could only have one, if, for some perverse reason I had to give up listening to him or looking at him, I'd give up looking. No question.

Yes, Harry is beautiful and charming and hilarious and all the other things. But if I didn't love his music, if it didn't move me, if it hadn't literally changed my life, I wouldn't be part of this fandom. And I certainly wouldn't be writing this book.

But it's hard to write about music when you can't quote lyrics. Actually, that may not be true for everyone. But certainly for me, the lyrics are so important that I can't really imagine how I can write about the songs without quoting them.

And I definitely can't quote them. Because it would cost a bunch of money. In the original draft of my first novel, I had the love interest sing a bit of McFly's *All About You* to my main character. It was cute and romantic and it was nine words. I emailed McFly's music publisher to ask what it would cost to use the line. It wasn't a lot, but if the book was translated or reprinted I'd have to pay every time and so I decided against it. Instead I had to say 'as he sang about dancing on the kitchen tiles…'. So, excuse me for any paraphrased lyrics you're about to read as I've tried to put into words how I feel about some of his songs and I've also asked a bunch of fandom friends what their favourite Harry song is and why.

For Kat, this is an almost impossible question:

> My first instinct was to yell 'ALL OF THEM', and then I wanted to list like four songs from each of his albums. But when I really thought about it, I was able to narrow it down to three songs, one from each album, that still surprise me each time I hear them. I also took into consideration the songs that I still get excited about seeing live, even after dozens of concerts.

Kat has seen Harry live – brace yourself – forty-two times.

'I made myself listen to these three songs this morning and confirmed that they, among all the other brilliance, still do something to my cells. I can feel myself becoming calmer and happier: *Ever Since New York*, *Adore You*, *Satellite*.'

Dr Louie Valencia can't choose either:

> Honestly, this is the hardest question for me. It really depends on my mood. If I'm wanting a little groove in my step to start the day, it would be *Music for a Sushi*

> *Restaurant*. If I'm in my feels a little, it might be *Two Ghosts* or *Sign of the Times*. If I'm feeling a little rebellious, maybe *Woman*. If I want to boost my spirits, maybe *Canyon Moon* or *Lights Up*. *Adore You* and *Watermelon Sugar* are comfort food!

This is something I too appreciate about Harry – there's a song for every vibe, every mood, every emotion. I've screamed along to *Kiwi* and cried along to *Falling*, dancing to *Daydreaming* in between.

The songs that open shows always become particularly special. I can't hear *Ever Since New York* without being swept right back to those early theatre shows. The pink, floral curtain falling and the guitar kicking in. Singing along with the chorus and feeling like … *this is it. I am here. We are here together.* There's nothing like it.

Adore You is the kind of song I would have expected from Harry out of the post-1D gate. If that had been his first solo song, I don't think I would have been surprised. (In fact, I've been surprised by the first new song from all three albums.)

For Michael, *Adore You* is quintessentially Harry. 'It's so much about love and loving and celebrating someone on a higher frequency, that's what pop music should be about: big, broad emotions.'

'It's a perfect pop song,' Becky agrees:

> It never fails to make me feel brighter or put a spring in my step on a rubbish day. If I'm happy, I'll play it; if I need a kick up the arse, I'll play it. It also reminds me of that moment after lockdown when we were finally allowed to see friends outside. I have the best memories of the sun being out, this playing loud in my garden and almost in tears because I was so grateful to be dancing like an idiot with my friends again. I'll always remember it.

For so many of us, *Fine Line* will always be indelibly linked with the lockdowns of 2020 and 2021. After the album came out, someone on social media worked out what time you would need to start playing *Fine Line* – the song – in order that the 'we'll be alright' line would play as the year changed over. I did this, at home with my family who were engaged in their own New Year pursuits and it felt hopeful. Of course, the new year was 2020 and just three months later the entire world changed, rendering everyone's '2020 vision' memes horribly ironic.

'I listened to *Fine Line* pretty obsessively through 2020,' Lynsey told me, 'and it provided a really cheering soundtrack to a very uncertain time.'

It was the same for Sophie. 'I listened to *Fine Line* a lot during lockdown and my very little daughter would laugh at the noises Harry makes at the end of the Sunflower Vol. 6. And now, every single time I hear those noises, I think of her little 2-year-old laugh and it makes me so happy. Lockdown was really hard, especially with such young children, but the album got me through it and makes me feel grateful to Harry.'

In *From the Dining Table*, Harry sings about playing with himself, alone in a hotel room. Overhearing me listening to it, my son Joe, 7 at the time, asked what Harry meant. I can only assume he was picturing a heartbreaking game of hide and seek. I told him the terrible truth. Joe, perturbed, said, 'Well, I don't know why he'd put that in a song …'

Lonely self-love sessions aside (or perhaps included), I appreciate that Harry is so open and vulnerable in his music. In interviews, he's generally pretty adept at saying nothing at all (although this did not serve him well during *Don't Worry Darling* promo) and while I know that all songs aren't autobiographical and he doesn't write them alone, he manages to communicate plenty.

In *Sweet Creature* he tells us he's stubborn. In *To Be So Lonely*, he references his arrogance. *Cherry*, his selfishness (and also pettiness –

the line about his former lover's new man's parents' gallery made me gasp the first time I heard it).

I know that *Woman* isn't a particular fan favourite – a friend said it's because it's too self-consciously sexy, like he's trying too hard – but I loved it from the spoken opening line. I love the sensual sway of the melody, only slightly undermined by the sound effect that Harry's stepdad Robin said sounded like the quack of a duck. It also contains the lyric I'm most likely to get tattooed (despite it being a Bukowski quote). To me it's about growing into myself and allowing myself indulgences and joy.

For me, *Only Angel* is the try-hard song with the worst lyrics on the album (I'm sure you don't need me to tell you which lines I'm thinking of) and I was surprised when a few people I spoke to chose it as their favourite of all Harry's songs.

'I love it so much as a song, but the real reason I call it my favourite is because of the emotional attachment I have to it,' Lexy told me.

> When I first saw him back in 2018, he opened with *Only Angel* and I truly had an out of body experience. Then, I saw him a second time in 2021 and he sang *Only Angel* right in front of me and it really felt like we had a moment … It sounds so silly, but I just adore hearing that song live and I have formed such an attachment to it that I have to call it my favourite!

While I didn't expect *Only Angel* to be anyone's favourite, I wasn't surprised by people choosing *Fine Line*.

'I love the soft drama of it,' Tewsday said, 'and its description of a non-straightforward love. That song and that album as a whole really speaks to the part of me that feels like my love doesn't need to be perfect or make sense to anybody else to be big and real.'

'It's like Harry and the band reached into my brain and my soul and pulled out all of the things that touch me most in a song to create it,' Martina told me.

> It starts so humbly small, and gets so gloriously big – that build up is all of my musical dreams put together. When he sings that we'll be alright, emphasised by the horns and strings and vocal embellishments and epic soaring bass notes – it's the most triumphant and triumphal outro to a song. And then it ends, with the whimper of a piano, and every single time I listen to it, still, after hundreds of listens, it still leaves me breathless and exhausted – in the best possible way.

From the opening notes, *She* almost gives me butterflies. When *Fine Line* came out, I went to a Harry pop-up in Camden and as *She* started to play, I thought 'Oh my god, I love this song!' before realising which song it was and also that obviously it would be playing at a promotional event for the actual album. I can feel the bass in my chest. I love the gentleness in Harry's voice, the falsetto in the chorus. Usually I'm not a fan of extended guitar noodling – I once fell asleep standing up at a Prince gig – but Mitch's guitar solo remains thrilling.

The first time I heard *Treat People With Kindness*, I laughed out loud. I couldn't believe Harry had actually made a TPWK song. And that it was cheesy as hell. I love that he did. I love that he just leans right into the cheese. I love that someone, at some point, came up with a boot scoot line dance to do during the shows. I love that I learned it but barely managed to do it – the first time I got sucked into a conga instead, the second time I kept forgetting one step and got confused while the friend I was with cackled at me. But I really wanted to do it, I wanted to be part of it! I love that Harry's friends and manager were filmed doing it. And I love that Harry did it himself at the final show of the tour.

For Tabitha Carvan, it's become something of a family anthem. 'We have a rule that when it comes on, you have to stop what you're doing and dance.'

Kiwi holds a special place in Lucy James's heart because at her first Harry show she caught the Pride flag he threw into the crowd.

'It's now in my family home in a picture frame with my ticket from the event, wristband from the pit and a photo of him waving it earlier in the concert.'

For Becky, *Falling* has a stillness and honesty to it. 'It's the perfect companion at 1am when you're feeling like shit. It's someone saying, "I've fucked up again" or "I'm not okay again" and I think most people can relate to that and the frustration when you've made the same mistake again.'

'My favourite song is *Boyfriends*, and has been since I got up at 7am and dragged my duvet to the sofa for the first night (morning) of Harrychella,' Ava told me. 'The whole set was very worth the early wake up, but *Boyfriends* floored me. I've heard him say he hopes that's the song people will still be coming to hear in fifty years' time, and yes. I think so.'

'As someone who lives an ocean away from my own family and siblings, *Sweet Creature* always reminds me of home,' Jen Wilde said. 'I know a lot of people think that song is about a romantic relationship, but to me it always felt like it was about his sister, Gemma, and their bond as siblings.' (Gemma did actually confirm on Twitter/X that *Sweet Creature* was written about her.)

My friend Rochelle chose *Little Freak*, 'because it has such Aquarius vibes'. I didn't really know what that meant, so I asked her to explain. 'As an Aquarius myself, it feels like the little things I might notice in someone else and liking the quirky things about them and acknowledging my quirky things. But also being super non-committal and being like I don't actually care who you're with when we probably do care.'

I love how the gentle, almost lullaby, quality of the melody contrasts with the lyrics. And how it's transformed when Harry plays it live and the fans go hard on the birthmark line. Throwing your head back and bellowing a single, anticipated line along with thousands of other fans is always thrilling. See also: the line about being an arrogant son of a bitch in *To Be So Lonely*, which, at the Los Angeles one night only performance of *Fine Line*, Harry pointed out the fans sang with their whole chest. I appreciate that Harry is always willing to join in and be part of the bit, throwing his arms wide and letting the fans sing it out together.

When the lyrics of Harry's former bandmate Louis Tomlinson's song about his mum's death, *Two of Us*, were leaked online, I cried reading them. I remember seeing someone tweet that the song had helped her access some residual grief she hadn't even realised was there and it's the same for me. I think for me it's the line about him seeing her again. I can talk about my parents' deaths quite easily and relatively unemotionally, unless I say that I can't believe they're never coming back. I don't think I've ever said that without my voice breaking.

A couple of friends picked *Matilda* as their favourite song, but said that it was too personal to talk about publicly. That's the thing about *Matilda*. The lyrics are sad, of course, but it's the gentleness and empathy that cracks my heart open. During the later shows, fans started releasing heart-shaped balloons during this song. As Harry sang – backed by the sweet harmonies from bandmates Sarah, Elin, Madi – he watched them fly away.

'Seeing people feel seen is such a special thing to me,' Ava said, 'and *Matilda* does that. I have full body goosebumps right now just thinking about it.'

When Harry's third album, *Harry's House*, was announced, I was in the process of selling the only home I'd ever owned and moving back to the town I grew up in and left at 18 when I made the move to London. I'd lived in that house for seventeen years; my two sons were born there. It was a big change. An exciting one, but nerve-wracking too. It felt auspicious to me that Harry was putting out an album about, as far as we knew from the online clues, the meaning of home.

The first single, *As It Was*, was released on the day we moved. I wasn't completely sold to begin with. I think, in some way,

I'd expected it to resonate with all the emotions I was feeling around the move, our new life. Which was, let's face it, highly unlikely to happen. As much as Harry's in my head, I have to remember I'm not in his. Still, I played it over and over, waiting to really feel it.

I'm not sure at what point I did start to really feel it, but it soon became my second favourite Harry song. I listen to it pretty much every day. It reminds me of making a big, brave move. And also it's a banger.

Funnily enough, my absolute favourite song of Harry's I didn't get on first listen either. On the day *Lights Up* dropped, I woke in the early hours, groggily shoved one earbud into my ear and blinked at my phone screen to be faced with flashes of Harry's chest, oiled, tattooed, tinged with green that put me in mind of the eighties TV version of *The Incredible Hulk*. The song seemed to be over before it had really begun. It felt to me like a prelude rather than a full song. I was, I admit, disappointed.

What I did find interesting though was that it was so unlike what I'd been expecting. As with *Sign of the Times*, I found myself thinking that I didn't know what I'd been expecting, it just wasn't *that*.

Same again with *As It Was*. It was unexpected. Different. But also, somehow, utterly, recognisably Harry.

And then the more I listened to it, the more I loved it. In the *Rolling Stone* ranking of all of Harry's songs, Rob Sheffield wrote that *Lights Up* 'captures the moment when you step into the light and finally recognise your true self', which goes a long way to explaining why it means so much to me.

Chapter Seven

Love on Tour

The moment the pre-show music stops. Darkness. Screams. A millennial pink curtain covered with flowers falls. A screen slowly rises.

Harry appears.

Frenetic, joyful, LOUD LOUD LOUD.

There's really nothing like it.

A Harry Styles show is literally one of the Merriam-Webster dictionary's examples for the definition of euphoria.

'Are you all feeling emotionally stable?' Harry asks the crowd at the Frankfurt show.

Crowd: Nooooo.

'Correct. You've come to the right place. You're in safe hands.'

I've seen a lot of singers and bands live since that first Bucks Fizz concert in 1982. Madonna, Michael Jackson, Prince. Bon Jovi, U2, INXS. George Michael, Whitney Houston, Diana Ross. Kylie Minogue, Duran Duran, Stevie Wonder. I've never experienced anything like a Harry Styles show. 'There's nothing remotely threatening, dangerous or intimidating about Harry,' Martina says. 'I've never felt as safe and joyful and seen at a concert.'

Collective effervescence.

A boot scoot, a conga line, a mosh pit. And the thing that makes the biggest difference is that Harry's having just as much fun as the crowd.

From pausing the show so a pregnant fan could go and pee and not miss anything to chatting with sleepy children – at his St Paul show in 2018, he shushed the audience when he noticed a toddler had nodded off – to searching the enormous Manchester crowd for his childhood teacher (he found her), Harry makes everyone feel welcome. This is intentional, as Molly Hawkins, his Creative Director, explained on a podcast: 'He really wanted people to feel welcome from the beginning. He wanted to welcome people into his world.' All that and also he's funny. Like properly laugh out loud funny.

Ava agrees:

> The man is an off-the-cuff comedy genius, and so many famous Harry moments, the stuff of memes and fan legend, have come from his reactions to his audiences, and the signs they bring. It's a thing of real joy, and he knows that, and plays off it. Many of his quotes become tour through-lines, with fans prompting him completely unsubtly until he comes out with one of his classics, all of them in on the joke. That, as much as knowing all the words to As It Was, is a beacon; a way for fans to be able to recognise each other. Imagine a private joke, shared between millions of people all over the world. We don't need to imagine, do we? We have loads of them.

There's a TikTok I love by British singer/songwriter Zoe Harmony, singing along to Harry songs, but adding all of the show moments the fans join in with, whether you've actually been to a show (or seventeen) or watched live streams or even clips on TikTok. 'Everybody put your hands in the air.' Harry responding 'Okay!' after *Adore You*. The Satellite stomps. And ending with the whale – the end of the show moment when Harry blows a mouthful of water in the air.

I rarely comment on TikTok, but I commented on this one to say that the previous day, I'd caught myself thanking an imaginary crowd in my kitchen while *Golden* was playing. Another time, listening to *Meet Me in the Hallway*, I set off through my house to do something and stopped in my own hallway with a feeling of déjà vu, before realising I'd unconsciously headed off at the exact time Harry would leave the main stage and walk to the B stage.

I hadn't thought of these moments as a private joke, shared between millions, as Ava said, but that's absolutely right and I love it.

I saw Harry twice on his first, small, tour. Looking around at the 90,000 people Wembley crowd towards the end of Love on Tour 2023, I couldn't quite believe I'd been lucky enough to see him in a 3,500-capacity venue.

(I still envy friends who got to go to the small preview show Harry did at The Garage in London, with its capacity of 600, the audience is doubled by dozens of tiny faces appearing on phone screens as fans FaceTimed friends to share the joy. The videos are both lovely and slightly uncanny – these little floating, bodyless heads, laughing, crying, singing along.)

The first shows were so wildly different to Love on Tour and even the 2018 arena shows. They represent Harry finding his feet, working out who he wants to be. It's pretty incredible to watch now, knowing the artist he's become.

And of course, I think back to the me of 2017. I was married. My kids were so much younger. 2016 had been terrible in so many ways – Brexit, Trump, the loss of so many beloved artists from David Bowie to Prince to George Michael – but none of us had any idea what would happen in 2020. It was truly a different world.

Yet watching this show, I can access how I felt at the time. I knew I was changing. I didn't know exactly what I was going to do, how different my life would be just a year on, but this tour, these songs, were there at the start, pointing the way to a whole new life. I'll always appreciate that.

I'd bought tickets for the arena shows before the small shows had even taken place. By the time they came around, I'd separated from my husband and decided to go all in.

Birmingham. Manchester. London. Glasgow. New York.

The arena tour saw the inclusion of two new songs, *Anna* – with its nod to George Michael's *Faith*, perfectly tailored to me – and *Medicine*, which instantly became iconic thanks to lyrical references to sexual experimentation – David Lindquist from *The Indianapolis Star* called it 'a raw-power ode to giving in to pleasure' – not to mention Harry's salacious delivery. (If by some chance you don't know what I'm talking about, search 'Medicine (St Paul)' on YouTube; it's the one with five million views.)

In Glasgow, as the screen slowly rose and I squinted, trying to work out exactly what he was wearing, my friend grabbed my arm. She was saying something, but I couldn't hear her over the screaming. She shook my arm, she seemed excited. The screaming was even louder than usual, but I still couldn't work out what he was wearing. Socks? Was he wearing knee socks? Wait. Yes. He (and as it transpired, his entire band) were wearing kilts. I laughed out loud. Of course they were.

I'd seen him at Glasgow's SEC Armadillo the previous year, on his first, small, tour. That night someone had shouted 'Where's your kilt?'

'Where's my kilt?' Harry had responded. 'I'm saving it for later, darling.'

And the crowd, inevitably, went wild.

This time, at the OVO Hydro Arena, not only was he wearing the promised kilt, he said, 'Before you ask, the answer is no' in reference to the tradition that a true Scotsman wears nothing under his kilt. (But did he mean, no, I'm not wearing any underwear or no, I'm not going commando? I guess we'll never know. But my money's on the first because he's nothing if not a massive tease.)

Later, between songs, he took a banana out of his sporran, peeled and ate it, and then pulled out an orange that he threw to the crowd.

(Real ones were reminded of the 2013 VMAs where Harry was seen seat-dancing behind Rihanna, while casually and methodically peeling an orange he proceeded to eat. He'd found it in a lift, apparently. Standard.)

It's not just the cherry, kiwi, watermelon references in his songs that inspired fans to nickname him 'Fruitman'.

'Please feel free to do whatever you wanna do in here … within reason,' Harry said before one of his shows. 'Please feel free to be whoever it is you've always wanted to be without reason.'

After my separation, before the tour, I bought a small white and rose gold enamel pin with the words 'Fall in love with yourself'. Every time I wore it, someone (always a woman) commented on it. Travelling for the Harry shows and spending time with fandom friends helped me fall in love with myself. (Back in the UK, the pin fell off and got run over by a car. I chose not to see it as an omen.)

While the community, the friends, the shared experience is of course fantastic, for some of my happiest tour moments, I was alone. A coffee in Seattle Airport. Flying over Mount Rainier. Watching New York wake up from the balcony of my Airbnb. Listening to Adam Buxton's podcast as I walked around New York (including the interminable treks through Times Square-42nd Street). Playing *Rainbow* by Kacey Musgraves so much that now it sounds like sitting on the subway and looking at my reflection in the window opposite. A wildly expensive glass of wine in New York when I wasn't ready for the night to end. Skipping down the subway steps, Metrocard in hand, and feeling like the kind of person who buggers off to New York for the weekend. Who has a Metrocard and knows how to use it (I'd had to google it when I first arrived and even then I found it pretty confusing). Here am I in New York, I thought. With my Metrocard. About to get the subway to go and meet my friends and then see Harry Styles.

It felt right. I felt happy and relaxed and free.

Later, walking up to Madison Square Garden, I looked up at the huge Harry billboard and felt proud. None of his achievements are anything to do with me. He doesn't know me. I don't know him. And yet. Look at him! In New York! At Madison Square Garden.

And look at me! I'm here. I made it.

I went to the second New York show with a friend who'd never seen Harry before. I was so excited for her to experience it. At the end, she grabbed my arm and yelled, 'He's so good!' I know! Other friends were planning to fly to LA for the last two shows of the tour and I was wildly envious. 'Would be so cool to go to LA,' I mused as we left the venue.

I made my way back to my Airbnb in pouring rain. I took a selfie on the subway platform. My hair is soaked and straggly. My glasses partially steamed up and dotted with drips. I'm wearing pink wired headphones. And I look as happy as I've ever seen myself look.

The following morning, I woke up and picked up my phone. I had a message from Andi, the friend I'd gone to the show with. She'd bought tickets for the final show in LA. In three weeks. She said if it turned out we couldn't go, she would sell them. I didn't think I could go. I couldn't afford the plane fare, for one, and it was unlikely that I'd be able to arrange childcare. I texted my ex to check. He said it wouldn't be a problem. I flew home. I worried about money. I looked at flights and they weren't that bad. And then Andi offered to pay for my flight and I could pay her back.

And so we were going to the final show.

Welcome to the final show

By the third encore of *Kiwi*, I was regretting taking off my bra. I decided early on that I didn't want to be distracted by discomfort, or spend the next ninety minutes adjusting myself, so I crouched down (during *Carolina*), whipped it through my sleeves and tucked it in my bag. If I'd known about *Kiwi* cubed I might've reconsidered, but part of the deal with Harry live is feeling free and I certainly felt free. Too free.

But before Kiwi, Harry gathered his band in a circle on the B stage – a lot closer to our seats than the main stage – and they started to play *Girl Crush* and I, a 47-year-old (braless) mother of two, clambered up onto a wobbly folding chair in order to film it for myself.

At my first ever Bros concert at the Manchester Apollo in 1988, my sister and I climbed onto our chairs and a member of staff hit us on the back of the legs with a poster tube. No one hit me at the Harry show, but my wobbly, blurry, video was probably not worth the risk.

And yet it makes me laugh when I think about it. What compelled me to climb up? I rarely watch the video I filmed so I don't think it was that. I think it was that I was in the moment. And I wanted to be in it more. I couldn't really see and I needed to see because it was the final show and he was singing *Girl Crush* with his band on the B stage. And it was great.

Love on Tour

After the theatre tour and the arena tour, after the pandemic delay, Love On Tour launched Harry to a whole new level.

One of the Top 5 highest grossing tours of all time, Love on Tour broke the record for the highest monthly attendance in Billboard Boxscore history, with 967k tickets sold. It raised over $6.5million for charity partners including Planned Parenthood, Save the Children and Every Town for Gun Safety, and became the show to be seen at for numerous celebrities.

Lenny Kravitz, Jon Bon Jovi, Madonna, Hilary Duff, John Mayer, Hugh Jackman, Florence Welch, Tessa Thompson, Barbie Ferreira, Nina Dobrev, Christian Bale, Drew Barrymore, Jimmy Fallon, Lizzo,

Hayley Bieber, Kendall Jenner, Kylie Jenner, Kris Jenner, Noah Beck, Sofia Carson, Millie Bobby Brown, Noah Schnapp, Dawn O'Porter, Joe Jonas, Sophie Turner, Jonathan Groff, Dave Grohl, Bad Bunny, Baz Lurhmann, Gwen Stefani, Tom Hanks, Halsey, Sara Bareilles, Ben Platt, Busy Phillips, Katy Perry, Orlando Bloom, Jeff Bezos, Rosé and Jennie from Blackpink, Rami Malek, Tate McRae, Mel C, Emma Bunton, Beto O'Rourke, Shawn Mendes, BTS, Ellen DeGeneres, Portia de Rossi, Stanley Tucci, Amelia Dimoldenberg, Bono, Maya Jama, Asif Ali, David Beckham, Stormzy, SZA, Lizzo, Julie Bowen, Meghan Trainor, Emily Blunt, John Krasinski, Jennifer Aniston, Emma Corrin, Pedro Almodóvar, Alexa Chung, James Corden, Nick Grimshaw, and more I've likely missed, all took in a show. Oh and Niall Horan.

Actor Jensen Ackles took his daughters and afterwards perfectly described the incredible exchange of energy between Harry and the audience. 'He is up there because he absolutely 100 per cent is loving every second of it,' he said. 'I hope we all get to feel like that.'

In March 2022, I suggested in the group chat that I might buy a ticket to see Harry in Australia early the following year. I've always wanted to go to Australia – in the eighties I was so obsessed with *Home and Away* and *Neighbours* that I watched both the new lunchtime episode and the teatime repeat of the same episode every single day; there's literally scenes I can recite thirty-plus years on – but I hadn't previously been able to justify (or afford) it.

If I did go, I asked, would anyone want to come with me? All but one said yes (she would, but she works for a university and it would be term time) and, the thing is, we actually did it. Kat, Lucinda, Martina, Syndea and me. Two of us from the UK, two from the US and Martina was already out there. (Because it's where she lives.)

We flew to Melbourne, stayed in an Airbnb with a rooftop pool with incredible views, did a bunch of tourist things and then saw Harry at Marvel Stadium, where the two girls behind us were seeing

This page and overleaf pages: Love on Tour, Manila, 2023. (Matt Jabez Alvarez)

Jingle Ball with One Direction, Dallas, 2018. (EmilyPixels)

On the Road Again tour with One Direction, Baltimore, 2015. (EmilyPixels)

On the Road Again tour with One Direction; Boston, 2015. (EmilyPixels)

Live on Tour, Dallas, 2018. (EmilyPixels)

Live on Tour, Hershey, PA, 2018. (EmilyPixels)

Live on Tour, Los Angeles, 2018. (EmilyPixels)

Love on Tour, Los Angeles, 2021. (EmilyPixels)

Love on Tour, Long Island, 2021. (EmilyPixels)

Love on Tour, London, 2022. (EmilyPixels)

Capital Summertime Ball, London, 2022. (EmilyPixels)

Love on Tour, Los Angeles, 2023. (EmilyPixels)

Love on Tour, London, 2023. (EmilyPixels)

Love on Tour, Los Angeles, 2022. (EmilyPixels)

him for the first time and screamed so aggressively, I was genuinely worried they'd tear their throats.

More tourist things including a wine tasting and me falling over in a rainforest (unrelated to the wine) and then a road trip to Sydney, hundreds of kangaroos, the Harbour Bridge and the Opera House, and two more hilarious, joyful Harry shows, with the second Sydney show adding *Horses* by Daryl Braithwaite to the list of songs that remind me more of Harry shows than Harry's own songs do. (See also *I Know a Place* by MUNA and *Supermarket* by Wet Leg.)

We were all there because of Harry Styles. Of course, we arranged the trip ourselves. We paid for it ourselves. But if not for Harry Styles we wouldn't have been there. If not for One Direction, we wouldn't even know each other – two of us are British, two American (from different coasts), one Australian. We became friends online because of a boyband and then we met – in New York, LA, Lancashire – because of Harry Styles. Isn't that a wondrous thing?

I found Tara Knight when a friend posted one of her Instagram Reels in our group chat. The reel showed Tara's young daughter wearing Harry inspired outfits while travelling to shows. Tara and her daughter live in Australia and travelled to the UK to see Harry. I live in the UK and travelled to Australia to see Harry. I slid into Tara's DMs to say hi, we both went halfway around the world for shows, but in opposite directions! And to ask her how this all came about.

In 2021, Tara had finished a contract role and decided to have the rest of the year off to spend time with her daughter, Evalee, before she started school.

'We were spending a lot of time in the car driving to and from the beach and going on adventures and I was letting her pick our music,' Tara told me. 'She discovered Harry and we both kind of fell in love. His music brought us so close, it was like a shared little secret just between us, and it became the backing sound for the most wonderful summer.'

Tara tells me that the trip to the UK was one of the best things she's ever done:

> It was incredible. Watching Evalee see Harry live for the first time (after watching a lot of dodgy live streams) it is hard to put into words. The whole experience, flying to countries neither of us had been to, getting dressed up, having people recognise her and want her photo, it was all so surreal.

And just to add icing to the Harry tour cake, in Glasgow they bumped into Harry's stylist, Harry Lambert, who signed a poster for Evalee.

Like Tara, travelling to see Harry was easily one of the best things I've ever done, so of course I had to do it again.

In Paris, Lucinda and I had floor tickets – my first time at a stadium for Harry – and another friend was seated up in the stands. During the pre-show, we chatted by text. 'Where are you guys?' Syndea messaged. 'In the big space on the left. Near a couple of bananas.' And she saw us. And waved. And we waved back. Thank you to those bananas.

The bananas in question were two young people with a quite startling amount of energy. Particularly since it was a hot evening and they were, you know, dressed as bananas. The Parisian bananas danced and sang. They jumped up and down, holding hands. They were all-in and apparently having the time of their lives. And they were doing it dressed as bananas. Why? Good question. I'm not sure where it started, but someone, somewhere turned up to a show dressed as a banana and Harry inevitably made up a song about it. ("Loving these bananas" Nick Grimshaw captioned a video he posted on Instagram of two dancing bananas in the crowd at one of Harry's 2023 Wembley shows. Same bananas? Who knows.)

One of the best things about the shows is how there are so many little moments that the fans pick up on from dance moves to quips to, during *As It Was*, bellowing 'Leave America' with such force that it could be heard literally miles from the various stadiums. Turning around and seeing the girls all backing up and opening a circle ready to rush into the centre for a mosh pit made me feel giddy with joy.

By the end of the tour, I'd seen on TikTok that some fans had started to lie on the ground during certain songs. Sometimes *Fine Line*, sometimes *Sign of the Times*, sometimes *Matilda*. In Paris, during *Fine Line*, I joined them.

I wanted a different perspective. I wanted to focus on the music, on the moment, to look up at the stars and think about where I was and why. Unfortunately, because I'm me, I mostly thought about how my bra wasn't supportive enough. I worried, because this is the world now, that someone would be filming me, and I'd become TikTok famous/infamous for lying on my back at a Harry show with my boobs in my armpits and not being able to get back up again. But the few times I did manage to quiet my ridiculous mind, I stared at the upside-down fans, at the phone torch lights in the stands, at the deep blue sky beyond. I listened to Harry singing that we'll be alright and I thought … Yes. That feeling of being in the right place at the right time, doing exactly what you're meant to do. Even if that's lying on the ground surrounded by thousands of other people.

In July 2023, in Reggio Emilia, Harry performed the final show of Love on Tour, ending with a ten-minute piano song he'd written especially for the show. It was so unexpected – he'd never even played piano on stage before – which made it, according to poet Bebe Ashley, all the more moving.

'It was a quiet moment of acceptance that these past few years have been long and tough and difficult but we've also all grown and found ourselves a little bit more.'

It's been thrilling to watch Harry evolve from the early intimate theatre shows to the stadium spectacles of Love on Tour. But, like Bebe says, the fans have evolved too. We're never just there for Harry, we're there for each other. Whether it's the boot scoot or the conga, the outfits or the costumes, the feathers from the boas every-fucking-where.

At a couple of shows, I noticed how often many of the fans weren't even looking at the stage; they were looking at each other. Singing to each other. Filming themselves singing to each other.

'I remember some young girls taking a million selfies in front of us and eye rolling at that,' my friend Andi said, 'but then I realised that they weren't doing anything to bother me and were in fact just enjoying themselves 100 per cent. I have really learned to not be judgmental and to enjoy other people's happiness in what they love.'

In Paris, just in front of me, a girl in cherry-printed white dungarees dropped to her knees about to play Mitch's *Fine Line* solo on air guitar. One of her friends waited, phone trained on her, poised to capture the moment. The cherry girl started playing a few bars too soon and all the girls all stopped dead, shocked to have messed up, and then dissolved into so much laughter that I'm pretty sure they missed the rest of the song.

I wish I'd been filming them. At Wembley in 2022, I took a photo of two fans on the row in front, arms around each other, singing and swaying, lost in the moment. When the show ended, I showed them the photo on my phone, Airdropped it to them. I took my older son's camera with me to Australia, ostensibly to take better photos of the shows. It was actually rubbish in low light, but it took brilliant photos of the crowd, thousands of pink and yellow and blue dots, fluttering with feathers and sprinkled with cowboy hats, thrown into giddy relief against the white of the ground.

'We holler and scream and shush and croon right along on cue,' Sophie Brookover writes in a 2018 piece called *I Stan A Legend of The Joyful Jet Engine*.

> We hold aloft our flashlight phones. We document all our favourite moments, for a whole bunch of reasons: our shaky, emoji-laden videos let us brag a bit, let us share the experience with those near & far, to confirm we really saw what we think we saw, to lay claim to a performance, to make space for ourselves IN the performance, to influence the performance and its history, to place ourselves AS the performer, and as the performer's fans.

We do. We do all of that. And it's an enormous part of the point of going to shows. Not just Harry's, but anyone's. Lately, though, there's been something else much less fun and sometimes actively dangerous. Fans throwing objects at artists isn't a recent trend – One Direction fans will remember Niall Horan getting hit with an iPhone in his already-injured knee – but it does seem to have escalated lately.

The astonishing popularity of TikTok has created a demand for content and an unexpected reaction from your fave can take you viral.

In an article for Mashable, Chase DiBenedetto suggests the cause is a combination of a new, social media-based concert culture, along with an intense competitiveness among those attending. And the competitiveness – the attempt to catch the hottest, funniest, weirdest moment – isn't limited to within your own fandom.

'It's more like a competition with the entire internet,' Chase writes.

Harry has always condoned if not encouraged the fun side of this impulse – picking up hats or glasses thrown onto the stage and wearing them for a moment before chucking them back into the crowd, posing with and singing to Harry dolls, cardboard cut-outs, teddies made in his image. At the O2 in 2018, a fan was throwing Haribo sweets onto the stage and Harry challenged them to throw one – just one! – that he would try to catch in his mouth. And he did it. It was amazing and hilarious and I'm happy I was there to witness it.

But during his 2022, fifteen-show residency at The Forum in LA, someone threw a Skittle, the small, hard, famously rainbow-coloured sweet, and it hit him directly in the eye. The video of the incident is genuinely upsetting. Harry's running down the catwalk when he rears back before immediately doubling over to press a hand over his eye. He continues shouting his thanks to the crowd, but only after gingerly touching his eyelid with his fingertips, as if to check for damage, and then keeping it squinted shut.

The Skittles brand account tweeted: 'Didn't think I needed to say this: Don't throw Skittles.'

Skittlegate was one in a stream of incidents of fans throwing objects on stage, often causing the artist to pause the show and worse. Bebe Rexha was hit in the face with a phone during a concert in New York. She suffered a black eye and the man who threw the phone was arrested.

Always forthright, Adele stated in no uncertain terms that she won't tolerate this behaviour. During one of her Vegas residency shows she asked if anyone had noticed that people have forgotten show etiquette, saying, 'They're just throwing shit on stage!' She made her feelings about this clear: 'Fucking dare you. Dare you to throw something at me.'

Country singer Kelsea Ballerini was also hit in the eye with a friendship bracelet thrown by a fan and, in an interview on the *Today Show*, said it was not only scary, but also took away from the concert experience.

'The point of live music and of live shows is escapism,' she said. 'It's connection and it's all being together and not having anything come in and obstruct that.'

It's interesting that Ballerini mentions connection, because I do think that for some fans, throwing an object at their fave is an attempt at exactly that. If you can't touch your fave directly, can you touch him indirectly? Can you force a reaction no one's ever seen before, even if it's a negative one?

♫ ♫ ♫ ♫ ♫

I didn't attend the final show of Love On Tour. Reggio Emilia, Italy, June 2023. I wish I could have been there. The beloved American YouTuber and entrepreneur Hank Green, once tweeted: 'I want a life where I can fly to Oregon to see Harry Styles with three day's [*sic*] notice.' I thought about it a lot in the run-up to that last show. The tour had been going for more than two years at that point and of course I'd already been to a bunch of shows. But the last one. In Italy. I want that life.

Instead, I watched it via someone's Instagram live, intermittently texting with friends who were also watching and wishing they could be there. The live was fantastic, the person filming not holding back from their own response, screaming, yelling, singing, at one point actually sobbing and then laughing at themselves for doing so.

It was almost as good as being there.

'Whatever this feeling is that you feel in this crowd tonight, I feel it,' Harry said in his emotional final speech. 'What you create together … it is the most inspiring thing I've ever seen in my life.

'None of you are alone. Look around, look at how many people there are here. We're all the same.'

I asked my friends about their experiences of seeing Harry live.

Amy Whitear

> I honestly didn't have very high expectations for a first solo arena tour but it was far better than I could've anticipated. Just 20,000 people sharing a very specific moment in time. It's hard to describe that emotion. I also saw him at Wembley, in a much bigger crowd on his never-ending tour, which I went to solo. I can't think of many live concert experiences I've had where it doesn't matter how you turn up – solo, in a small group, with

friends or family – you end up totally absorbed in a crowd, making friends with total strangers and baring your soul to them when you start sobbing during Sign of the Times. Doing the conga, choking on boa feathers, the catharsis of screaming certain lyrics from the top of your lungs.

I love live music, and I think Harry in particular is great at creating an environment where you can just be free and enjoy yourself and lose yourself in the full sensory experience without fear or judgement.

Katie, Running Water Tattoo

I saw Harry live four times and every show was surreal. I wasn't a fan, hadn't listened to him when I saw him for the first time. He was all over my TikTok and was playing fifteen nights in LA, so I just wanted to see what the hype was about.

I don't like going to shows when I don't know most of the songs but I was completely blown away even before the show started. When *Best Song Ever* started playing and the whole stadium knew the lyrics and the whole pit was dancing the choreography I was just standing there in shock. I'd never seen anything like this and it only got better and better.

The feeling of community and belonging was insane. Harry's inclusivity and the way he makes everyone feel welcomed and seen and safe. The way everybody's dressed similarly, the way everybody watches him, his every move, his interaction with the fans and reading the signs – it felt like it was one big family and everyone was a part of it. Not just an artist on stage and an audience watching the show, but artist and fans as a unit.

Jen Wilde

Being disabled and more at risk of Covid, I didn't go to any Love On Tour shows, but I went to one of his Madison Square Garden shows in 2018. I didn't have much money so I ended up sitting in the clouds, almost behind the stage, but I still had a great view of Harry waving his Pride flags. Unfortunately, I was there with my (now ex-) girlfriend, who wasn't a big fan, and spent the whole night seated next to me, texting and making comments about how we were too old to be there. One day, I hope to go to a Harry concert again, this time with my wife, who will sing and dance with me all night long.

Lucy James

I think if I count the One Direction shows I've been to as well as Harry's solo shows I've seen him perform live ten times (which compared to some in the fandom are rookie numbers).

During the 2023 leg of Love on Tour I went to five shows. People who aren't huge fans didn't quite understand why I was going to the same show five times but it wasn't just about the show it was about the atmosphere and experience as well as getting to share the space with Harry. He has a way of performing that makes each show feel unique even if it's the same set list with the occasional change. (At Slane Castle, he sang *Little Freak* which wasn't on the permanent set list; a small win for me, as it meant I'd heard every song from his three albums live!)

I can truly say I had the summer of a lifetime and may or may not have already started saving for next tour!

Dr Louie Valencia

I saw One Direction five times, and I've seen Harry solo something like thirteen times … To say the least, there are a lot of experiences there to talk about. For me, what makes a Harry Styles concert special is knowing you are going to a place where people can feel love – from Harry, from fellow fans, for yourself. I think my favourite show was probably in Manchester in 2022. I left completely exhausted, and spent the day in a daze with other fans, burning in the sun. What I love most is seeing people feel comfortable to express themselves and to 'be whomever they want to be'. The following day, I went to Holmes Chapel and got to see where he grew up – which was very special.'

Sa'iyda Shabazz-Ryne

I have seen him eleven times and every single one of them is burned in my memory. Harry Styles's concerts feel like a giant homecoming; even if you're in a room full of strangers, there's a safety and feeling of comfort and community when you're there. Plus it's SO MUCH FUN. The joy! The glitter! The feathers!

Becky Peacock

I've never been to a stadium gig before and seen so many groups of fans interacting with each other. I was with my best friend – and we're women in our mid-thirties – but we ended up chatting to and singing with tons of young fans. There's a freeness and joy we felt that I wish you could bottle and take home. It's probably the warmest fandom I've ever experienced. Just a huge bunch of people being unapologetic about what they love and the delight in sharing that as a collective. That feeling absolutely comes from Harry.

Syndea

Although I'm trying to describe it, it's honestly indescribably joyful. The first time I saw him, I just couldn't believe I'd managed to get to this place: from watching him on my laptop endlessly to personally experiencing him do a cover of *Still the One* with Kasey Musgraves. Still one of my lifetime happiest concert moments.

Connor

I'd been watching videos of Harry doing this tour for the last two years, so it's not as if there were any surprises, but somehow I was still very emotional. I found myself crying more than once and I couldn't fully understand why. I absolutely loved the colour and the joy of the crowd. We were way nearer to Harry than I thought we'd be and it was a little bit like a religious experience. In fact, I was continually reminded of when I had gone to youth rallies with Pope John Paul II as a teenager. There was fervour and there was happiness and yet it all felt very wholesome and very safe.

Lynsey Rogers

I went on my own but dressed up in my best glittery, rainbow and heart-themed things. The atmosphere was buzzing and so friendly; everyone was there to have a good time and look out for each other.

I sat near the back (I can't stand for long periods) and worried it would feel too distant, but the atmosphere, use of the screens and the spectacle of the show melted away my worries. Yes, he was a very small pink sparkly dot to me, but the most gorgeous pink sparkly dot! I had a blast and ended up dancing most of the night away. Everyone around me was up on their feet too, but it was nice to sit back for more reflective moments and soak up the emotion.

For such a huge show, it really managed to feel intimate, like a party! Harry's energy and magnetism makes it feel like an immersive experience; that's such a rare and special quality. I can see why people get hooked on his shows. There's still such a misogynistic culture around music fandom and it's so affirming to be around other people just as passionate as you are!

As a queer person, the fact that his shows always open with a message of feeling safe and being able to truly be yourself means a lot. It's not often you can switch off and fully immerse yourself in an experience, but it's always a joy when that can happen; the crowd are united in their love for the music and having a great time. Honestly, sometimes you just need that shortcut of seeing a flag or hearing a reaffirming message to know that this is a space for you.

Lindsay Bown

A massive part of the experience of seeing Harry live, for me, has been sharing those special times with people I love so much. I can specifically remember probably the most joyful moment I have ever had, at the Manchester show. It was just after the conga line broke up and we ended up in an open space dancing like crazy and it felt amazing. Really, really freeing. And I remember thinking 'this is how Harry wants us to feel at his shows. Just like this. Free to be whoever we want to be.' It was fucking awesome.

Sophie

I suffered with anxiety in the 2010s and never went to see One Direction live, which I really regret. No one would go with me and I was too scared to go on my own. This year I went to two Harry Styles concerts on my own and I've met the most wonderful people. I know it's not good to have regrets but I do regret that a lot.

The first time I saw Harry live was when he first went solo. I remember that I was a new mum – I'd given birth about four months before the show – and I pumped my breast milk before the show! I went with a friend who created a One Direction podcast, it was so nice to meet her in real life, and we had a brilliant time dancing together.

The second time I went to see Harry was just after lockdown ended. I hadn't been in London since before the pandemic. I was very excited to see him, and so happy. I'd been counting the days! But when we were about to go inside Wembley Stadium, I had a rush of anxiety. I was completely full of panic. The friend I was with was so calm and so kind; we walked around outside till I felt ready to go in. I was shaking. When we got to our seats, the venue was playing *Best Song Ever* and the girls in our section were doing the dance and I joined in! There was this unspoken bond between us all and I got goosebumps! I knew I was with my people and everything was going to be okay.

Someone I know works with people who live with addiction, and said that no matter where they are, an AA meeting will feel like home. Even if they're in a completely different country. That's how I feel at Harry Styles concert. I know I'm safe, I know everyone around me will understand how I'm thinking and feeling. I know I won't be judged for dancing badly, or crying, or screaming, or doing all of these things at the same time.

While Harry toured the world in early 2023 I kept up with all the shows on YouTube. I loved seeing all the different concerts. When Harry played in Coventry, I was feeling excited because he was the closest he'd been to me in months! I sent my best friend a text as I was going home at around 5pm. It said, 'Harry Styles is literally two hours away from me, and I wish I could be there so much!' And my friend replied with 'check your email'. So I checked my email and they had sent me a ticket for that very night!

I raced home, confirmed that my husband was okay to look after my girls, and off I went! I was so completely unprepared. But I did it. I drove all the way to Coventry by myself and I got onto the pitch just as *Bohemian Rhapsody* was playing. I was on my own, I felt so safe and so happy and I couldn't stop crying. They were tears of happiness but also tears of pride because I'd done something really brave. And I cried because I have a friend who believes in me so much they sent me a ticket to see Harry.

Amy Miller

I've never felt more safe or more happy at one of his shows and it really feels like a celebratory environment every single time. He's so entertaining and endearing. He wants to keep you entertained and keep you on your toes but he is also very aware of what we want and what the nostalgia of little moments from his One Direction days mean to us and he incorporates it all. It's really special.

Bebe Ashley

My book *Gold Light Shining* was published in October 2020, so I had managed to get tickets to shows in Philadelphia, Harryween [in New York], Birmingham, London, Vienna, Budapest and Dublin, and had all these great and mad plans to take the book on a mini celebration tour. Because of the pandemic, all these shows were cancelled.

I finally saw him play Slane Castle in 2023. As soon as he ran out on stage I started crying. I'd waited three years since my book was published to wave it around in the same air that he was singing in and I was just so happy! It was a beautiful venue, a natural amphitheatre, with 80,000 people there just having the best time.

Kat Hazzard

The first time I saw him solo was September 2017; San Francisco at the famous Fillmore Theatre. That show established it all for me – my obsession with his tour wardrobe eras, his touring band that became a part of my fandom experience almost as much as Harry was; the way that the Harry fans expanded and morphed from former 1D fans into strictly solo 'Harries'; the 'Treat People With Kindness' vibe of the live shows, even from the beginning before TPWK was a single and a way of life; the eternal safe space that can always be found at any Harry live performance – it all grew from those initial smaller venues in the last quarter of 2017. I got to see Harry perform at the famous Ryman in Nashville; got to hear his singular voice in that hallowed sacred space. Those 2017 shows were pretty magical.

2018's Live On Tour shows were even more magical because I threw caution to the wind and travelled all over the US and Europe meeting up with friends that I'd made on the internet. I guess I should've been scared meeting up with total strangers whom I only knew by their photo/ avatar and not usually even their real name on a social media platform, but I wasn't apprehensive at all. Many of these people whom I met in the summer of 2018 have gone on to become best friends who I can't imagine not having in my life. The February 2023 trip I took to Australia that I spent with four of these amazing friends, where we travelled through Victoria and New South Wales to see Harry styles perform in huge 70+ thousand capacity stadiums was one of the most magical trips of my life.

Michael Lee Richardson

I never got to see One Direction on tour, so my first time seeing Harry live was in 2017, when he was touring the first album. My friend Claire and I went to see him together, she always tells this story about how she was flying to Berlin the next day, and woke up with basically no voice, and then when she saw my Instagram Stories she realised why – during *Medicine*, when Harry sang the line about 'the boys and the girls', Claire screamed, 'Yes, Harry!' it was what can only be described as an ear-splitting volume. It was glorious.

That show solidified something that I love about Harry: I've never seen a popstar so at home in himself and his own sexiness, when he's performing he's like something from another dimension, but all his between-song banter is straight out of Batley Social Club. "Hiya, y'alright?" It's beautiful.

At the start of the show, fans were handing out pieces of coloured paper and asking us to put them over our phone torches and turn them on during *Sign of the Times*. When we did, it created this rainbow around the whole stadium. It takes a lot to make me cry, and I can be cynical about these things and what they mean, but it was genuinely moving, all the more so because it had come from fans themselves.

He also wore a kilt. It was disgusting (in the best possible way).

I saw Harry again at the Love on Tour Glasgow show with a friend who's much more of a 'boy's music' fan, he'd never been to a pop show before, and never been to a gig of that size or scale, and the reaction he had was so lovely. He talked about how he'd never been in a crowd that big and not felt threatened before! That show was amazing: we were up in the stands, up in the gods, and not everyone can fill that kind of space – I love popstars, I love pop shows, but I've been to stadium gigs with huge stars who just couldn't reach the back row – but it still felt like we were part of something, it was brilliant.

Andrea Knapp

Just seeing Harry be so completely opening himself up to the crowds, being RAW in his emotions was something new. I mean you see stars talk to their audiences, but his was the first concert that I felt a genuine one-on-one connection with and I wasn't even the one he was talking to. He appears to enjoy everything he does and it oozes from every pore.

Martina Medica

I saw him live in Melbourne by myself the first time, and it was one of the best nights of my life. Being surrounded by girls, women, and members of the LGBTQ community with him and his band on stage was just the most joyous, blissful experience. It was a room full of joy and love and laughter and music and tears and there was such amazing reciprocity between him/the band and the audience.

Helen Wood

It's like adult Disneyland, going to his shows. Leave reality at home and just be happy.

Ava Eldred

I've seen Harry live twice, which feels quite lightweight considering I spent my teenage years following boybands, and find so much joy in adult fandom because so many of the barriers that were there when I was younger have been removed. Maybe next tour is the one! The first time I was weirdly nervous – there was so much pressure on it, having waited two years and most of a global pandemic to get there – our lives had changed completely in the time since I'd booked the tickets, but this touch point from before had never stopped being exciting, and we'd put glitter on our faces, and got the train to Wembley, and it was finally happening. It had to be amazing. And it was! Of course it was! It was also over far too quickly for something that had been such a long time coming, and I wanted more crowd interaction! More encores!

More time to soak it all in! I will probably remember that moment where the heavens opened as he sang *Sign of the Times* for the rest of my life, though. It felt designed. If I wrote it, an editor might say it felt too earnest, but it happened and it was perfect.

The second time I was far more relaxed, and perhaps I'm projecting (I don't think I am) but so was Harry. It was a year later, and he was a year more experienced. That was one of my favourite gigs I've been to. Someone asked me the next day how it had been, and I said 'He's really learned to do a stadium show. I can't wait to see how good he's going to get.' He's an absolute natural, and don't get me wrong, is already spectacular – one of the best live performers currently touring, for sure, but I have this feeling that there's so much we haven't seen yet. So much more joy to come.

Chapter Eight

Ur Mum

The first time I saw George Michael live, on his Faith tour in 1988, I went with my sister, she's two years younger. Literally my only memory of the entire show is of her screaming directly in my ear. It hurt. I think I smacked her? I know I was furious. *I mean, God, there's literally no need to scream, is there?* I didn't buy it. For me, it wasn't an expression of excitement or joy, it was attention-seeking. And really fucking annoying.

But what if I was wrong? What if she *was* freely expressing her joy and I was the repressed one, worried about how it looked (sounded), afraid to, you know, let myself go. I'm going to take a leap and say that was exactly the case. I was 17. The oldest, the responsible one. Trying to control everything, including myself.

One of the women Tabitha Carvan spoke to about Benedict Cumberbatch compared Tabitha's feelings for Benedict to how some women feel about horses, saying 'It's about finding a way to lose control.' Tabitha reacted in the same way I would, by wondering why anyone would want to lose control.

The Harry shows are probably the closest I get, but a) I've discovered that it takes two drinks (more and, yes, I can really let rip, but then I don't remember much about the show and the following day is a write-off), and b) I'm still probably only at about 70 per cent on the loss-of-control scale. And of course the weed gummy I had at the Met Gala viewing party I threw with my friends only succeeded in making me even more anxious than usual.

'Who were we screaming at?' Sophie Brookover asked in an article about seeing Harry live:

> It wasn't only at Harry Styles, Actual Person, or to the stage iteration of Harry Styles, Famous Person. We were screaming it to each other, to ourselves, to people not present who we wish were present. This is why we scream at pop stars. We need to take our emotions and put them somewhere.

I think perhaps my concern is that wherever I put my emotions, screaming would let them out. And then where would I be?

In her 2019 Ted Talk, 'For the love of fangirls', Yve Blake talks about how she became obsessed with the way fans scream at concerts. She talks about research done by Carol Gilligan (along with Lyn Mikel Brown) on how between the ages of 11 and 13, girls begin to perform and alter their voices, deepening them to sound more serious, less feminine. Boys, on the other hand, begin to perform and alter their voices at around 4 years old, because that's when they learn that crying and squealing are not manly.

And so screaming, for girls, represents a time before they learned they had to modify their behaviour to be taken seriously in the world. And they do it, Yve says, without apology or fear.

At the end of her talk, Yve gets the audience to stand up and scream. It's thrilling.

British indie rock group Wet Leg were the support act for many of Harry's 2023 shows and during their song *Ur Mum*, they encouraged everyone to scream. Like properly, literally, scream. Almost everyone did and I loved it. I loved that even at a Harry show where much of the audience is going to be screaming for much of the time, it still felt radical to encourage everyone, all these girls, these young women, to release their emotions, to feel that freedom. I felt so happy and grateful that Harry had chosen Wet Leg as his support and that I was there to witness it.

I didn't scream though.

I don't think I've ever screamed. I don't even know how I would go about it. I've yelled, of course. I've whooped. But I genuinely can't even scream in my dreams (I try sometimes but no sound comes out). During *Ur Mum* would have been the perfect time to do it, or at least attempt it. But I was self-conscious. If I'm going to scream – and I'm still not saying I am – I don't know that I'm going to do it in front of strangers, even ones I know (hope) won't judge.

Through her Benedict Cumberbatch fandom, as she writes in her book, Tabitha learned how to let herself lose control. And at the Harry shows, she screamed when Wet Leg told her to scream. It was a life-changing experience, she told me.

And I'd missed out on it.

Mad Woman

In the summer of 2023, my eldest son sent me a video of fans singing and dancing in a circle at a cinema screening of Taylor Swift's Eras tour and compared it to *Midsommar*, the 2019 folk horror film about a Swedish cult.

Back in 2013, before I knew anything about One Direction, I saw on Twitter that Louis Tomlinson had taken part in a match for his beloved football team, Doncaster Rovers, in aid of a children's hospice. Reports stated that the stadium had been 'flooded' with thousands of One Direction fans and some of the male supporters were less than impressed.

I'd already been aware of the difference in how people judge female fandoms, particularly boyband fandoms, and sport fandoms, but here was a direct comparison. It was perfect! The teenage girls – screaming in their One Direction T-shirts – are fanatical, obsessed (whisper it: hysterical). But the men? They're just passionate about the Beautiful Game.

Back then, I was delighted with myself to have made that connection, but over the next few years I was to read it again and again. I heard it on a podcast just yesterday, the hosts joking about girls going to see Harry Styles versus men going to football and what if there was a football team made up of eleven Harry Styles? The comparison is laboured and yet I keep coming back to it.

Men are allowed sport fandom, even when it includes some of the worst behaviours. Research by the University of Lancaster found that violent domestic abuse incidents increase by 38 per cent when the England team loses and by 26 per cent when the team wins or draws.

But, yes, the girls dancing in a circle to Taylor Swift are the ones we should be afraid of.

'Things that women are passionate about are pathologized and infantilised and otherised in a way that things men are passionate about or not,' Tabitha said when I talked to her about this. And then she blew my mind by pointing out how Taylor Swift's relationship with American football player Travis Kelce brought the two fandoms together. Another direct comparison. And the Taylor fans were of course more open to the football than the football fans were to Taylor with many NFL fans believing her to be a distraction at best, booing shots of her on the Jumbotron and claiming she's 'ruined football'. (Her power!)

Much of the criticism has come from conspiracy theorists, who claimed Swift and Kelce's relationship was fake and contrived to boost the NFL, or Covid vaccines (Kelce appeared in adverts promoting Pfizer's vaccine), or Joe Biden's re-election campaign (Swift endorsed Biden in 2020), or all three.

The Taylor effect reportedly boosted the brand value of the NFL (National Football League) generally and the Kansas City Chiefs (Kelce's team) specifically by $331m (£260m) and particularly, unsurprisingly, with young women. Sales of Kelce's replica jersey spiked by 400 per cent after she first attended one of his games.

In her dissertation, Lucy James addresses some of the similarities between sport and music fandoms through the lens of their parallels to the formation of a cultural identity through religious practice.

She points out the similarity between fan 'uniforms' – the feather boa is to the Harry Styles fandom what the replica jerseys or kits are to sports fans. 'They are both affirmations of the fan identity and, in turn, an individual's cultural identity,' James writes.

I thought about this when I first read about fans at Louis Tomlinson's Doncaster games. How are the One Direction T-shirts any different – less valid, more vapid – than the replica team shirts the Doncaster supporters wore? That's not a rhetorical question. They're simply not. The only difference is the interests of girls and women are taken less seriously than the interests of boys and men.

For once, I wanted a man's opinion, so I messaged my friend Paul and he suggested we talk on the phone like it was 1990. But I agreed. Paul is 50 and runs a fan club for UK supporters of an American football team, the Cincinnati Bengals. Despite having almost no crossover in our music tastes (I asked him his opinion of Harry and it is a testament to our friendship that I didn't immediately block him after reading his response; 'deathly dull middle-of-the-road pop' indeed), we talked about fandom and sexism, passion and obsession for almost an hour.

Like me, Paul is well aware of the wildly different ways people think of female and male fandoms.

'If men have a passion they carry over from their childhood or teens, it's sweet and cool and interesting, whereas for women it's often considered unhinged.'

I was intrigued that he'd used the word 'passion', just as I was when Angie, my Beatles cushion companion, said it. I tend to use the word 'obsessed', but even to me it feels more loaded than 'passionate' does.

So I did a little experiment. A Google image search for 'hysterical fans' results in a page full of photos of girls and women, mouths open in screams, hands pressed to faces or stretching out towards the objects of their affection. They're fans of The Beatles, Elvis, BTS, Hanson. And, of course, One Direction.

The results for 'obsessive fans' are similar, but with additional references to the 'bizarre habits' of fans, the 'dark side' of fandom and one photo labelling the pictured One Direction fans as 'over-emotional'.

Finally, I typed in 'passionate fans'. Can you guess the result? Even though I expected it, I was still shocked. (How I can still be shocked at this point, I do not know.) Football. American football. British football.

I googled the definitions. Obsession versus passion. Passion, you'll be relieved to learn, is healthy. It helps you to reach your goals and follow your dreams. Obsession, however, is apparently more likely to derail them. If you're obsessed, you can't think about anything else. You start prioritising your obsession over other activities and commitments. You're addicted. You're out of control.

It once again comes down to women's interests being widely considered less important, more frivolous, than men's. As Alicia Lansom wrote for Refinery29 in 2023, 'Groups of women who enjoy boy bands are defined as "hysterical" because the art they've chosen to love is deemed unworthy of such a reaction.'

Only unworthy, of course, until men become interested.

Often the music industry treats teenage girls as the most lucrative audience but also the least respected. They want their money (or their parents' money) but nothing else.

In a 2015 *Rolling Stone* profile, Australian band 5 Seconds of Summer's Ashton Irwin said, 'We don't want to just be, like, for girls. We want to be for everyone.'

For everyone is great, an admirable goal. But I wonder if he'd be concerned if their appeal had been limited to just, like, boys. During an interview on Alan Carr's *Chatty Man*, after Alan tells them they are the most-requested guests the show had ever had, Ashton Irwin says their record label describes them as 'the biggest band that no one's heard of'. Their millions of fans were clearly well aware of them, so you can only assume the record company meant 'no one who counts'.

As Tabitha Carvan writes in her book, 'We had so much love to give, but it wasn't worth anything coming from us.'

I was interested to know if male fans feel this too, so I asked TikTok creator Dan Cash. He has, of course, always been in the minority when it comes to One Direction and Harry Styles fandom and I wondered if he's taken more seriously than female fans. I've fallen into this trap myself in the past – the fact that Rob Sheffield loves Harry gives him that little extra frisson of credibility, not just because he writes for *Rolling Stone* and knows his music, but because he's a 'proper' music fan (albeit one who has been obsessed with Duran Duran for forty plus years). Dan Cash told me:

> Even with making so much content about the band and Harry, I've never wanted to insert myself as some kind of authority in the fandom. I'm just another fan making content I enjoy making, talking to likeminded people.
>
> I remember back in the day, there were 'boy Directioners' and they were quite rare. One Direction was marketed towards girls, which I feel ostracised a male audience slightly. Most of my friends saw it as embarrassing that I was a huge fan. I never really cared and still don't. But I feel like the (incorrect) public perception of the band being for girls, and making cheesy pop music, and not being talented because it was all written for them and heavily autotuned, put a lot of people off.
>
> Fragile masculinity might play a part – men don't want to like things that are 'for women'. And the way Harry has challenged gender through clothing will put off the straight dude bro guy men, you know? It's all a

> load of nonsense. It's only been very recently that men in my life have opened themselves up to Harry's music and admitted to it being good.
>
> I do feel like I am received differently by the fandom because I'm a man. I get a lot less age shaming, I think. I'm not sure why. I see a lot of women sharing opinions and getting torn apart on Twitter, but I've never really had that. A couple of times, sure, but nowhere near the amount I've seen some female creators get. There are definitely examples of misogyny directed at some female creators or big fan accounts on Twitter – and also towards women in Harry's life. And it's surprising, because Harry is a feminist and loves women. His musical influences are women – just look at his relationship with Stevie Nicks and Shania Twain.

I've mentioned that my very first fandom was the seventies Scottish pop group, 'Tartan teen sensations', the Bay City Rollers.

I was 5 when they had their breakthrough hit, *Bye, Bye, Baby* so I think we can assume this fandom was thrust upon me, rather than being my own choice. I know I loved *Bye Bye Baby*, but the song I remember listening to even more was *Bay City Rollers We Love You* by The Tartan Horde. I think little me thought it was Bay City Rollers approved (for years, I misremembered it as the B-side to *Bye Bye Baby*).

Writing this book, I thought about this and considered it interesting that one of the first songs I loved and listened to over and over was by fans singing about how much they love their boys.

And then I googled it.

Bay City Rollers, We Love You was written by singer and songwriter Nick Lowe in an attempt to convince his record company United Artists to let him move to the much cooler Stiff Records. While it is a genuinely good, catchy song (Nick Lowe is, of course, a great songwriter), it wasn't intended to be a tribute to the Bay City Rollers or their fans. It was a piss-take.

And doesn't that just say it all. Boybands aren't to be taken seriously. Girl fans aren't to be taken seriously. They're so cringe that you can mock them in song to get your record label to let you move on to better, more credible, things.

♫ ♫ ♫ ♫ ♫

'I wish my mum would do that with me!'

We'd only just arrived at Old Trafford Cricket ground for Harry's June 2022 show when we found ourselves the centre of attention. Or rather, one of us did. My friend Lindsay had brought along her mum, Sylvia – who, at the time, was 70 years old – and a group of American fans were delighted to meet her, calling other girls over to chat and pose with Sylvia for selfies.

'I absolutely loved it,' says Sylvia now.

> I didn't feel in any way that I was being ridiculed. I was clearly a much older fan than most and for some reason that I can't quite fathom they seemed a bit fascinated. There were other older ladies there too, but [the girls] were drawn to me, perhaps I looked confident, happy and comfortable in my skin which is attractive I guess.

She definitely did. She's super glamorous, gregarious and always smiling.

Lindsay enjoyed her mum being singled out too. 'It made me feel really grateful for her and her willingness to say yes when I suggest a Harryventure.'

Almost everything I've read has positioned boyband fandom as something you do in your teens and grow out of. Why? Who needs uncomplicated joy more than middle-aged women?

In a 2017 article for *Buzzfeed News*, titled 'Aging Out of Diehard Fandom Is Bittersweet', Hanif Abdurraqib wrote about how fandom as an adult looks different, feels different, and is generally performed differently; he argues that this is because, in part, adults have so many more life commitments and therefore less time to engage in these passions.

'As an adult,' he writes. 'I've found my pop culture passions have had to serve as a brief and joyful escape.'

So it's not that we have to grow out of them for, I don't know, emotional development reasons. It's more the prosaic idea of being a grown up: you must give up what you love because you have to go out to work, pay taxes, and when did you last clean the washing machine filter?

On the one hand, this makes the 'brief and joyful escape' of fandom even more important. But on the other … why are we prioritising the washing machine filter/[fill in your specific personal household nemesis] over our own joy?

♫ ♫ ♫ ♫ ♫

At Johan Cruyff Arena in Amsterdam in 2023, a woman held a sign asking 'Am I too old to get your attention?'

'Never,' Harry reassured her from the stage.

A Harry update account on Instagram posted about the interaction, describing it as 'Harry affirming the Harriatrics.'

Harriatrics.

I don't feel great about that, I have to say.

Years ago, I saw a photo online of an elderly woman wearing a One Direction backpack. The comments were all about how cute it was but how it probably belonged to her granddaughter or how they doubted she even knew who One Direction were. I have a Harry tote bag that I take to Tesco. It chills me to think the staff or customers might be thinking 'Oh there's that old lady with her Harry bag', or that I'm just using it randomly and don't know who Harry is.

If anyone had ever asked, I planned to tell them I was writing a book about him. That's an acceptable reason. That's not weird. I've got this Harry tote (and the badges on my denim jacket and two tour T-shirts and a folder on my phone of future tattoo ideas) for professional reasons. So. Bet you feel silly now.

I know this is my own hang-up. I don't feel my age and so I still struggle when others see me as the middle-aged woman I absolutely am. At the airport, on the way back from LA in 2018, my friend and I went for something to eat. The entire time we were away, my friend chatted to and made friends with everyone. I've never known anyone so eager to talk to strangers. She told the server that we'd been in LA to see Harry and the server turned to me and asked her, 'And is this your mum?'

I am in fact old enough to be my friend's mum. Just about. But I didn't think I *looked* old enough to be her mum. (For much of my life, when I told someone my age, they'd be surprised. That's stopped now. I miss it.)

And again, like Gary Barlow yeeting (no, I'm not too old to use that word, shut up) me out of the make-up room back at *The Big Breakfast* in 1993, the server's question moved me away from being a fan having dinner with a friend and into a different category. Back then it was from insider to fan. In LA it felt like I'd been shifted from 'fan' to 'too old to be a fan'.

I saw an Instagram post from someone at a Harry show captioned 'Living out my 20s in my 60s! It's never too late!' And I agree. I really do. I want to say I don't feel like I'm in my fifties, but what is that even supposed to feel like?

Being an older fan doesn't bother Sylvia:

> Being older is a privilege, after all there isn't really any better alternative. I think us oldies feel we are allowed to like him because he wouldn't mind one bit. He isn't the kind to dismiss anyone at all and we feel as if we are

> equally as important to him as his younger fans. We are still here that's the main thing and can be bothered to enjoy this lovely human being.

Queen of the Harriatrics has to be Reina Lafantaisie, who, after a video her granddaughter filmed of the then 78-year-old waxing lyrical about Harry went viral, was invited to the Grammys to talk about what made her a superfan. On stage for the presentation of Album of the Year, Trevor Noah handed the card to Reina to read out. Arriving on stage to accept the award, Harry made a beeline for Reina, pulling her into a tight hug.

My friend Kimberley saw Harry first in Chicago and then in Paris. She took her almost 80-year-old mother, who didn't know Harry or his music, to both shows. 'We wore featherless boas and I sang along and enjoyed it but didn't feel as connected to him live as I thought I would. I think it was the huge crowd and the age of so many fans – teens and twenties. I felt a bit silly and out of place.'

Because of her age.

I totally get this and have had my own moments of 'what am I even doing?' at shows, but so far I've been able to talk myself out of it. What I'm doing is something that brings me joy and I refuse to feel bad about it. Also, bumping into Kimberley and her mum after the Paris show – somehow, out of 80,000 people, we ended up eating chips and drinking wine outside the same bar – is one of my favourite memories.

A few years ago, I saw a couple of my parents' friends – women in their seventies – for the first time in years, and they asked me what I was up to. I told them I was about to go and see Harry Styles in New York and they were both very excited.

'Harry Styles?' Audrey said, 'He's very dishy!'

(I love the word dishy.)

Dee – who was married to a musician and involved in the music industry in the sixties – told me how she frequently travelled to see a band she loved, The Overtones. How she would follow them on tour, meeting up with fellow fans at different shows and they'd all catch up with each other and the band together.

I felt like I'd seen my future and the thought of it made me happy. What could be better than travelling with your friends to do something you love, meeting new people and having new experiences? Why would anyone ever want to give that up?

I'll never be able to see Harry Styles with my mum, she died in 1999. We did go to one show together as adults, to see Barry Manilow at Wembley in 1996. And even though I've been to concerts with a friend and her mum, I hadn't thought about it being a thing. Not until Tabitha Carvan pointed it out to me.

'Mums who took their young daughters to One Direction concerts are now taking them to see Harry Styles,' she said when we spoke on Zoom. 'It will then be able to become a multi-generational experience with your daughter or your mother. And that is just like dads taking their sons fishing or to cricket or football.'

When I spoke to my friend Paul, he told me that he used to go to the football with his dad who went with *his* dad. Now he goes with his brother and his brother's son.

When I was pregnant with my eldest and we found out we were having a boy, we drove straight from the hospital to Ewood Park, home of Blackburn Rovers Football Club, to buy a replica shirt onesie for the future baby.

Football is often seen as a male family tradition and initiation into male rituals. Men sharing sport with their sons is a lovely thing, Tabitha says, 'But with female-centred interests, it is usually time-limited. You're a mother, you have to let it go.'

But what if you don't?

In the *Greatest Days* documentary, Ben Knowles, former news editor of *Smash Hits*, talks about Take That fandom as 'A love that's been passed down through generations.' The fans talk about the bonding experience of seeing the band together. Singer, TV presenter, and long-time Take That fan, Alesha Dixon, says she got to experience seeing the band with her mum and she's hoping to be able to experience it with her daughters too.

I asked Lindsay, who's been to a bunch of Harry shows with her mum, Sylvia, what she thinks about this.

'I've absolutely loved going to see Harry with Mum,' she told me.

> We have loads of happy memories of spending that time together and doing things we wouldn't otherwise have done. Especially visiting another city to see him, where we get to be totally present with each other and have real, in-depth conversations about life. Even things like spending a night together in a hotel and laughing about daft things in the early hours. When else would we have done that? Also, I love that she wants to come along with me and meet my friends and be part of everything. I think it keeps her really youthful and I know she feels really proud of that when she tells her friends about our adventures. We spend lots of time together generally but it's different when it's a Harry trip, seeing each other SO excited to see him is so joyful.

Dawn took her 14-year-old daughter to see Harry for her first ever concert and says she doesn't think the two of them would have both enjoyed any other concert as much.

'It felt very much like a safe space to take her to,' Dawn said. 'I can't think of any other act that would appeal to two different generations as much as Harry.'

Rochelle says her dad took her along to the more traditionally male activities, but seeing Harry with her two step-daughters and her sister reminded her of her mum taking her to see New Kids On The Block and the Backstreet Boys.

'Mom was super into that. And now it was my turn to do it,' Rochelle said. 'Only difference was that I wanted to see Harry just as badly as my nieces did.'

Mary's seen Harry five times with her daughter (and met me in the car park after the final Forum show in 2018, after we'd been online friends for years).

'I think my and my oldest daughter's shared music taste is a lot like the hyper-masculine stuff fathers and sons do,' she says. 'In fact, I feel like I'm closer to my older daughter than the younger because she and I really don't have any shared interests like that. It makes it harder for us to be on that sort of friend level.'

Ruth Broadway says that trying to find any opportunity to hang out with her 14-year-old daughter is something of a challenge. So she was happy to spend a day bonding over wearing feather boas, glitter face paint and matching Harry shirts.

'She sobbed through every song, bless her.'

'It's something that [Evalee and I] will continue to do together,' Tara Knight told me. 'It was such a fun adventure that we could share and it was so much fun meeting other mums and daughters creating the same memories.'

I know Lisa from my Bros days. She worked with the mum of friends I met outside Matt Goss's apartment and who used to come and wait for him with us. Lisa's been to see Harry twice with her daughter, Caitlin, and also took Caitlin to Holmes Chapel to visit the bakery that teen Harry had worked in.

Caitlin loves that her mum has always understood her obsessions because she's always had her own. They once waited twelve hours outside Shawn Mendes' hotel so Caitlin could meet him.

'None of my friends' mums would ever have done anything like that,' Caitlin says.

Even though I knew Mum was a Beatles fan and loved John Lennon – and even though I'd connected Mum's weird little John Lennon figure with my own weird little Harry Styles figure –

I somehow hadn't connected the idea of our fandoms. Or that Mum's Beatles fandom came along at an unhappy time, just like my first fandoms and just like my One Direction fandom.

I'd written a whole section about the idea of multi-generational fandom through the female line without recognising my own experience.

And then, towards the end of writing this book, The Beatles released their final song. Called *Now and Then*, the song was written by John Lennon in the seventies. Following his death, the demo he recorded was left unfinished for almost thirty years before being completed by surviving Beatles Paul McCartney and Ringo Starr, using guitar tracks recorded by George Harrison in 1995.

Scrolling Instagram one day, I spotted that The Jacaranda Club in Liverpool, site of the first performance of The Beatles before they were even called The Beatles, was inviting customers to come and listen to the first play of *Now and Then*. I went along with my 19-year-old. The club was absolutely rammed but we squeezed just inside the doors and listened to the last ever Beatles song, along with so many other fans. It was really emotional and it felt really special to share it with my son.

It wasn't until much later that I watched the music video for *Now and Then* and saw that it featured the older Beatles playing alongside their younger selves, similar to how the characters in *Greatest Days* sing with their younger selves.

♫ ♫ ♫ ♫ ♫

I genuinely believe that we shouldn't give up our passions, that you're never too old to do what you love … But then also I wonder if this all coincided with perimenopause? Is it hormonal? I've heard people describe menopause as 'reverse puberty' and puberty for me certainly involved a lot of yearning over popstars. (This morning I sent a friend a TikTok of a slideshow of photos of Harry Styles backed by a song including the line 'Is he hot or are you just ovulating?') Does it matter? Would that make it less real?

Sara Pascoe said that staring at the back of Robbie's head was the most powerful she's ever felt and that she doesn't feel that way about her husband. She's not staring at him doing the dishes trying to mentally will him to turn around and see her. What if, instead of being ashamed of these feelings, trying to explain them away as hormonal or hysterical, telling ourselves we have to grow out of them, what if we allowed ourselves to feel that power and trusted ourselves to use it for good. And by 'for good', I mean for making ourselves – allowing ourselves – to feel good.

Years ago, I read that PMS and perimenopause act as a sort of inner guidance system, trying to get us to pay attention to changes we need to make in our lives.

After being married for a while, I noticed that me and my ex would argue at the same time every month. Once I recognised that the fights were hormone-driven, I was able to stop them. But what if they were meant to happen? What if my body was trying to tell me that the marriage was no longer working for me?

But why do I feel the need to find an explanation?

In *This Is Not a Book About Benedict Cumberbatch*, Tabitha Carvan talks to a woman who, after becoming obsessed with the actor, took herself off to see a psychologist. As Tabitha says, 'Why does an objectively good thing, like a new passion, trigger an identity crisis?'

Tabitha told me:

> So many women read my book and then they write to me and confess that they have fallen for Harry Styles. But they always do it in this really apologetic way. They'll say, 'Even though I'm old enough to be his mother or his grandmother.' Or, 'I feel like I could look after him.' And I just feel profoundly that they do not need to do that.

> There's always something wrong with whatever it is that women like. They're too old or too young. They're too uncool. It has to be absolutely unimpeachably perfect to pass all these tests that we– mostly women, to be honest – put on ourselves. And that's why I just say go for it full throttle. Don't feel the need to explain it or apologise to anybody.

And I don't anymore. Mostly.

Chapter Nine

What the F is the X Factor?

I didn't watch *The X Factor* the year One Direction were formed and came third. I'd tried watching it the year before because everyone on Twitter seemed to be having fun and I felt left out, but I'd found it infuriating – no one, in my opinion, had any X factor at all. There were some decent singers, okay performers, sweet personalities, but I didn't see anything like charisma.

But obviously since falling into the 1D fandom I've watched the One Direction origin story and while many (if not most) of their performances are in retrospect – I'm sorry – pretty poor (with the exception of *Something About the Way You Look Tonight*) they absolutely had that indefinable something.

This has always fascinated me. People talk about boybands as being manufactured, but so often the industry tries to manufacture a boyband and it just doesn't work. You can't just pick a bunch of good-looking, talented boys and make a successful boyband. If you could, there'd be so many more of them. There's a fascinating BBC documentary from 1993 about a boyband called Upside Down. All the elements are there, but, for no apparent reason, the magic is not.

The documentary also brings up so many other interesting things – the boys' desperation for fame; their parents' concerns; everyone brushing away contractual worries because this may be their only chance; the absence of any concept of duty of care – legal, physical, emotional – to the boys; and the fact that they establish a fanbase, albeit small, immediately – girls are primed and ready for a new boyband, even one that doesn't actually work.

The origin of the term 'X factor' – which I hadn't even thought about until now – relates to algebra, where a single unknown in a simple formula is usually designated as an x. (All these years, I've been saying I've never needed to know algebra. And I still don't.) The X factor is something we don't conclusively know. But usage has evolved to include an indescribable quality. We know something is good, we just can't put into words *why* it's good.

Regarding Harry, I think by now we can put it into words how and why he's good – tens of thousands of them in this book, for a start – but there's still something ineffable. He has, as one friend put it, an electric energy that pulls you in.

'People say he's a female-written text,' Tabitha says. 'Like he's been created by women. I do think that is true. I think the way that he allows himself to be seen is the way that women want to see him.'

'It's about humility and kindness,' Martina says. 'Self-belief. A willingness to put himself out there, take risks, and risk failure. I personally think that a lot of what people call the X factor is really just a particular (and particularly strong) combination of those things.'

Or, as my friend Amy puts it, 'like he was engineered in a lab to be a popstar'.

While I was writing this book, I messaged a friend to ask about her favourite Harry Styles song. She replied with a video of him performing with Wet Leg, saying she loves how he is interested in so many different genres. When I scrolled back, I spotted that I hadn't asked her about her favourite Harry Styles song, I'd actually asked 'Do you have a favourite Harry Styles?' When I pointed this out, she said 'Please note that I just assumed it must be a thing and went along with it.'

At which point I realised it absolutely is a thing. There's *X Factor* Harry (often called foetus Harry or – and this may just be me and my friends – broccoli Harry). There's One Direction Harry. There's Italy Harry, Harryween Harry, Harry with kids, glasses Harry, behind the scenes in the studio Harry, model Harry, headband Harry, tight white jeans Harry, Japan

Harry generally, Japan dog friend Harry specifically, yacht Harry (so many yachts), karaoke Harry, drunk and/or high Harry, flirty with men Harry, wedding Harry, home for Christmas Harry, Hampstead ponds Harry.

There's a Harry for everyone.

Boyfriends

On *Late Night* with Seth Meyers in 2014, Jenny Slate said: 'I, as a teenager, wasn't so good at being a teenager; I'm good at being a teenager as an adult now.'

I have quoted her on this so many times, but I hadn't watched the entire clip. It turns out, she was telling a story about when she went back to her high school to give a speech at graduation. She talks about how a teenage boy came up to her and asked her to take a prom photo with him. And how she jumped at the chance, because when she was a teenager, the teen boys didn't like her and that feeling has never left her. So now, as a grown woman, she was so flattered to be chosen by a teen boy that she made it awkward.

A friend recently suggested that part of Harry's appeal is about people – and we know it's mostly girls and women – being allowed to be joyful and silly and brightly-coloured without shame, 'as the hot boy finally says it's okay and instead of looking down on you, celebrates and encourages it'.

I've thought a lot about the freedom of a Harry show. About having permission to be yourself. But I hadn't thought about who was giving permission (or if I did, I assumed I was giving myself permission). I hadn't thought of it in terms of validation from 'the hot boy'.

As a 2022 tweet put it, 'All this over a man … We should all be embarrassed.'

But while the hot boy may be the one on the stage, within the community of the fandom, he's almost entirely absent. All this is not about the man, not really, it's about the fans and from Bros to Take That to One Direction, they've almost all been women.

For Georgie it's more the feeling that you don't need the hot boy at all. 'You can have that kind of crazy fun with your friends and strangers-becoming-friends and you don't need to worry about being too cool or put together or trying to impress anyone.'

Ava sees it more as permission to celebrate authenticity.

> Sure, [Harry's] public persona is a heightened version of himself but it feels completely real, and I think that naturally trickles out into the fandom, and the wider world who appreciate him without considering themselves capital-f Fans. There is no blueprint for a Harry fan – we're all completely different despite our common interest, but at least in the areas of fandom that I've found myself in, that's accepted entirely with the understanding that everyone is being themselves. That they're able to be authentic because that's what Harry encourages. I'm certain it isn't universal – he's a man, not a superhero, and humans are complicated, but for the most part it seems that to be a fan of Harry is to be open, and accepting, and to actively attract new experiences and people with the same values.

Feel

In the Robbie Williams documentary, he and his wife Ayda both differentiate between 'Rob' the person and 'Robbie' the star. Stars are people too. But they're also not. And we don't want them to be, of course we don't. Or, as my friend Lucinda puts it: 'I don't want to know that Harry Styles is a real person.' Why doesn't she? 'Harry Styles the performer/personality/whatever is less fallible for not being a "real person".'

Kat feels differently. 'You know how when you're in love with or crushing on someone and you find yourself so endeared and overwhelmed that you earnestly want to find a flaw in them so that your adoration can simmer a bit? That's how I feel. And Harry is a young white dude! So there have been plenty of things that he's said or done that have filled this need for me.'

She wants him to do something to put her off? To make her less obsessed?

> Yes. Because to be honest, sometimes my love for Harry is overwhelming. For example, that period when he wore those godawful cream tasselled loafers was bad for my eyes but honestly great for my heart because the veil of perfection (that I put on him!) was lifted if only momentarily. Sometimes I can feel my fondness becoming too much so I try to think about things like the terrible loafers or mustachrry because I need something to dim his light for me.

I totally get that. But I don't want his light dimmed for me. I feel like there are enough dim lights. I want him to always shine.

Leather & Lace

Six a.m. on a Saturday in 2017, I woke up suddenly, picked up my phone and opened Twitter. And saw that while I'd been sleeping, Harry Styles had been on stage at the Troubadour in LA performing songs from his new album, but also, unbelievably, duetting with Stevie Nicks. I immediately burst into tears. I will always be overwhelmed watching people's dreams come true.

I was, admittedly, very much a latecomer to Fleetwood Mac. I was introduced to them via their eighties bangers, *Big Love*, *Little Lies*, *Everywhere*, and I knew there had been line-up changes and many inter-band relationship shenanigans, but I hadn't listened to them much. At that point, I didn't even own their seminal album, *Rumours*. But I knew Harry loved them, particularly Stevie.

Stevie performing on stage with Harry was a very big deal.

I made myself a cup of coffee and settled down to watch the videos. They sang *Landslide*, *Leather and Lace* and *Two Ghosts*. The fans lucky enough to be there cheered, screamed, sang along. They knew how important Stevie Nicks is. To music and to Harry.

'I'm, er …' he said once the two of them had finished singing, '…losing my shit'.

One of the things that most fascinates me about Harry Styles is how he always seems utterly present. It fascinates me because I do not have this skill; I am generally either worrying about the past or fretting about the future. If I'm experiencing something thrilling, I have to remind myself to stay in it, take it in, enjoy it. Something that seems – though obviously I don't know for sure – to come naturally to Harry.

As he sang with an icon, he patted his chest, threw his head back, eyes closed, appreciating the moment. Later, he blew out a breath, wiped his eyes, covered his face with his hands, laughed out loud, visibly overwhelmed. Stevie Nicks beamed at him, hugged him, rubbed his back, as present for him as he was for her.

Later, Stevie sang and Harry sat down on the edge of the stage and just watched, his eyes gleaming. Absolutely willing to give up his own stage, to become a fan at his own show.

Of everything Harry Styles has done, it's this Troubadour show I'm most envious of. Yes, I wish I could have been there, it must have been incredible to be in the audience at such an intimate show, so early in his solo career. Plus it's an iconic venue. But more than that, I wish I could have been on stage. I wish I could know what it feels like to make your dreams come true in that way. To feel the warmth and love from the crowd. To sing with your musical hero. To know that you are in the exact right place at the exact right time, doing exactly what you're meant to be doing.

In the Elton John biopic *Rocketman*, there's a scene where Elton performs at the Troubadour and it changes his life. He's singing, playing the piano, and the crowd is going wild. As he plays, his body floats up from the stage. His hands are still on the piano keys, but the rest of him is in the air, buoyed by the music, by the crowd, by his dreams coming true. It's a beautiful moment that made me cry in the cinema. After a few seconds, he slams back down to the stage in time with the crowd, but it's not a metaphor for coming back down to earth, it's about being present, in your body, in the world, knowing you're doing exactly what you're here to do. I'm never going to experience this from the stage (singing *Rainy Days and Mondays* in a town hall with the school choir didn't quite cut it) but I can experience it from the crowd.

And, it seems, one of the things Harry is here to do is to befriend even the prickliest celebrities and Forrest Gump his way through popular culture.

Saved on my phone I have a gif of Elton John on stage saying 'I love One Direction, fuck off', after he dedicated a song to Harry at one of his shows and the crowd booed. This was back in 2013 when it certainly wasn't as cool to like Harry as it (sometimes) is now.

When a fan asked Liam Gallagher on Twitter if it was true Harry once gave him a basket of fresh fish, of all things, Gallagher replied, 'Yes he's a crazy little guy.'

In fact, online, you can find collections of sweet things fellow celebrities have said about Harry over the years with Chris Martin's 'I'm pretty sure I was a straight guy before [seeing Harry]', being one of my favourites.

Stevie Nicks called Harry the son she and Mick Fleetwood never had. Mick himself has modelled nail polish for Harry's brand Pleasing, and called Harry 'a magical man'. The first time Harry met Stevie – backstage after a Fleetwood Mac show – he gave her a cake he'd baked himself. It's surely this kind of shit that makes everyone fall in love with him.

Before they were famous, Halsey was a huge One Direction fan, writing a song about Harry with lyrics that included fantasising about kissing him and memorising his fingertips. (I simply cannot imagine how embarrassing it would be to have written something like that about someone who subsequently became a peer.)

Even Harry's sister, Gemma, was stunned when he performed with Shania Twain at Coachella, tweeting that she couldn't fathom it, because they'd grown up listening to Shania in the car on repeat.

It was casually announced in 2023 that Harry had posed for a portrait by David Hockney (who it seems Harry met when he was hanging out at Joni Mitchell's house; of course he was hanging out at Joni Mitchell's house). The resulting portrait divided opinion, to say the least, but the fact that one of the most iconic painters wanted to paint Harry is quite incredible.

While as far as I know, I can't include former president Barack Obama as an official Harry friend or fan, he does feature in one of my very favourite fandom memes. In 2014, US tabloid the *National Enquirer* ran a small cover story claiming Obama had had an affair with a man. A One Direction fan for some reason photoshopped a picture of Harry over the original photo. The UK tabloids picked it up and ran it, apparently without even checking, as if it had been the *National Enquirer* story in the first place. And then, inevitably, the fans ran with it even further than most people could imagine, coining the ship name Hobama.

There are manips of Harry and Obama kissing. Of Harry pregnant and Obama smooching his belly; of Harry sitting in Obama's lap; Harry in an evening gown feeding Obama sushi. And my favourite, the two of them leaping towards each other, arms thrown back, chests out, toes pointed, like trapeze artists about to embrace, against a background of the American flag.

The fans wrote a forbidden love story for the former member of One Direction and the former president of the United States.

My favourite is a fanfic AU gifset 'President Obama falls for part white house intern part rockstar Harry Styles. Obama surprises Harry in the audience of one of his shows and the affair blossoms from there.' One gif shows Harry saying: 'I can't believe you came to see me', and then one of Obama captioned: 'I don't have the strength to stay away from you anymore.'

None of it is real. But don't you think it could be? Don't you wish it was?

One of the questions I asked everyone I spoke to for this book, was 'What do you love about Harry?'

Lindsay Bown

> I love how gentle and kind he is, that he has the ability to make connections with people so easily even in the midst of chaos. I've met one or two people like that before, those who have the gift of making you feel like you're the most fascinating person to be around and being under their gaze feels like pure sunshine. And it really is a gift. I love his authenticity, especially on stage, he is just being himself. And I love to see the joy that performing brings him – he's having the time of his life right now and it's wonderful to see. I love the way he dresses and have taken a little bit of style inspo from him, here and there. And his sense of humour. He makes me laugh a lot. I think ultimately, I love that he is just a Good Person. A Genuinely Good Person.

Tara Knight

> He has done incredible things for people and the environment all over the world but for me he allowed me the space to find exactly who I am, to not be ashamed of the type of memories I am creating with my daughter and to create friendships with people I would have otherwise never met and who I will cherish forever.

Sophie

What I love the most about Harry is that he's created a wonderful safe space for so many people who are anxious or have been marginalised and discriminated [against]. His concerts are so special and empowering for so many of us.

Amy Miller

Harry for me is very much softness personified. There's an openness and playfulness to him that I really seek out in people. A lot of the challenges in my life have been because of hardened people and when traumatic things happen to you because of someone else's cruelty, it can often harden you to the world and to men, especially. I've worked diligently to stay soft and open and really hold onto childlike magic and Harry really reflects that in such a special way.

Harry's made me feel incredibly brave to just … exist. I'm a very anxious, very scared person day to day. I'm very uncomfortable in my own skin and don't know how to be and so many of the moments where I've felt free and happy in myself has been at a Harry show. The last year, I've really pushed myself to carry that feeling throughout the rest of my life. I don't have to be beholden to only that space where I feel safe and free. I can become that space for myself and for others and hopefully it'll carry out beyond me. Harry reminds me what joy is and how infectious and powerful it can be.

Michael Lee Richardson

There's something so specific that I respond to in Harry and his music that it's hard to pin down, but I think it's about the fact that he's so comfortable in himself and his sexuality – I don't mean sexual orientation there, I don't care about his sexual orientation – there's something so soft about a lot of his songs, a lot of his lyrics are just about loving and celebrating the person he's with at that time, I just find that really appealing. When I've seen him perform, it's so much about bringing people – all people! – in, making them feel welcome, making them (us) feel part of something. The world can feel like such a scary, divided place, but at Harry shows and within Harry fandom, I feel like I'm part of something fun and exciting and cool, something bigger than myself.

Also sometimes he's so hot it makes me want to throw up.

Liz Harvatine

Of course, I don't know Harry personally, I can't speak to who he actually is, but I don't think that matters. I love the person I perceive him to be. The Harry I think I know is kind and respectful but funny and snarky at the same time. He's not a perfect person but he is willing to acknowledge his shortcomings and is open to growth and change. He cares about his family and friends, he cares about his fans and he cares about all of the people he works with and who work for him. I can't get enough of who he is, he's a delight. And if he's secretly a monster he's done an incredible job of hiding it because every bit of insight we get about who he is and how he treats people reinforces his reputation as a wonderful person.

Lexy Jones

This is a tough question because I truly like everything about him. But I think the most correct answer is his kindness. When I saw that Harry's tagline was 'treat people with kindness' I knew I was supporting the right person. This phrase has always stuck with me (I even have a tattoo of it now) and it has been an inspiration to me in more ways than one. I have made countless art pieces surrounding this phrase and it has now become a mantra of my everyday life.

Martina Medica

His silliness. His humour. His grin. His risk-taking with music, as a 'former boyband member'. His openness to new things. His absolute unending and unwavering kindness. His down-to-earthedness. His humility, in the face of extreme fame and fortune. His love for what he does. His love for his fans, and what they have brought to his life. His tattoos. His thighs. His fandom.

Sarra Manning

Yes, he's extraordinarily beautiful and he writes catchy songs, but I also think it's quite rare for someone with his level of fame and beauty, to (mostly) use his powers for good. I also like that he has such a special relationship with his fans and that the community that's built around him is a welcoming and inclusive space. It would probably be much easier for him to be an arsehole, but he seems like one of the good ones.

Chapter Ten

Treat People With Kindness

In his 2017 Apple Music documentary, Harry says he made an intentional choice to be more private, after feeling like everyone knew everything about him. Of course, that enthusiastic and unguarded openness from the *X Factor* days was surely part of his (and all of One Direction's) early appeal, but, as we know, Harry was 16 then. There is – and should be – a huge difference in what a 16-year-old wants and is willing to share online versus a 31-year-old.

Plus a certain air of mystery is often part of the persona of the biggest stars. We've all heard the ridiculous notion that 'we have the same twenty-four hours as Beyonce' which, yes, is factually true, but how often does Beyonce lose a chunk of those hours on hold with the Inland Revenue or doing the ironing? But even if she was doing that (she's not) we don't want to know about it. We like our biggest stars to be relatable … but not too relatable.

Michael argues:

> Popstars should feel like they've been beamed in from another dimension. They can be recognisable, but they should feel magic and weird and sexy and cool, they should feel aspirational and inspirational, they should always feel a bit unattainable and otherworldly. Harry is all those things, for me. In a lot of ways – especially here in the UK – he feels like the last of a dying breed of proper popstars that feel like they might have come from outer space. He's sort of defeated the odds, in that

> respect – he came from a reality TV show! – but we don't actually know that much about him. There's an element of mystery about him, a sense that people are making up their own lore, that's what a popstar should be, for me.

I remember, as a teen, realising that George Michael existed all the time, not just when I could see him. At the time I had that thought he was somewhere doing something and I didn't know what it was. I wanted to know. I still feel like that. Ideally, I would like Harry Styles to wear a headcam so I could just hang out with him, virtually, whenever I wanted. But of course I don't actually want that for him – I appreciate and accept that he's entitled to his privacy – but also for me. How would I ever get anything done?

TPWK

During the first tour, fans spotted a badge on Harry's guitar strap featuring the acronym 'TPWK', short for Treat People With Kindness. Before long, the slogan appeared on tour merchandise (I have a T-shirt) and was used in the teaser marketing campaign for the *Fine Line* album. Along came the song and the fabulous video in which Harry nails an Old Hollywood style dance routine with actress and writer Phoebe Waller-Bridge.

Building your brand around kindness is not nothing. And it's not like he doesn't practice it either, from what we know of him and how he moves through the world. Everyone who works with him, everyone who meets him talks about his kindness, his consideration, his generosity. (Okay, almost everyone. Per her recent memoir, Dame Joan Collins did not find him to be kind, recounting how, at the Met Gala after party, Harry stood on a table to watch Cher perform, blocking the dame's view of proceedings.)

Harry's guitarist and one of his closest friends, Mitch Rowland, said that when he and his wife Sarah, the utterly brilliant drummer in Harry's band, were planning to start a family, Harry gave them their own separate tour bus for privacy and space. They didn't ask, Harry offered.

The band MUNA, one of the support acts on Harry's 2017 theatre tour, said recently that Harry paid for everyone to have the same catering and ate in there with them every day.

The dancers at the Grammys, the models in his videos, even fans who have met him in the street, talk about his kindness. He seems to absolutely practice what he preaches. And, yes, you can say 'Treat people with kindness' doesn't go far enough, is wishy-washy, isn't explicit enough. But it's not nothing.

But on an episode of his podcast, Justin Hawkins, singer in rock band The Darkness said something that intrigued me. He said that always being nice is a way to disarm people. 'If you're always nice, they don't know anything about you.'

Which doesn't mean Harry's not nice, just that his niceness could in fact be an intentional way to protect his own peace.

Golden

'He has just kept on winning and winning,' Harry's sister Gemma wrote in her article for *Another Man* magazine. 'There's no denying he's golden.'

At least he was.

When I started writing this book, I had intended there to be a chapter about movie star Harry. But then the films came out …

Turns out there can be a downside to being a hugely successful, handsome, charismatic and charming celebrity. You're given opportunities that you wouldn't otherwise get and may not be ready for.

(Another downside is having your personal life wildly overshadow every aspect of the work.)

I don't think Harry was terrible in *Don't Worry Darling*, *My Policeman* or in his one minute appearance mid-credits of *The Eternals*. But I also don't think he was good. There were good moments, moments that suggested he could be good one day. And I think he shone in his first role in Christopher Nolan's *Dunkirk*. But I really wish he hadn't been given these later roles before he really knew what he was doing.

I would still love to see him in a romcom. Preferably one written by me. (Although I imagine I've ruled out that possibility with the above paragraph.) I think he'd be better if he wasn't trying to be intense and dramatic. Be sexy and funny and sweet and charming. We all know he can do that.

In 2023, Harry was nominated for six GRAMMY awards including Record of the Year, Song of the Year, Best Pop Solo Performance, and Best Music Video for *As It Was*, along with Best Pop Vocal Album and Album of the Year for *Harry's House*.

He won Album of the Year and, in his speech, said 'This doesn't happen to people like me very often …'

Considering he's exactly the kind of person this happens to (the last Black woman to win Album of the Year was Lauryn Hill for *The Miseducation of Lauryn Hill* in 1999), the backlash was swift and vociferous, with many claiming that, from the 2023 nominated artists, Harry was the least deserving and the award should have gone to Bad Bunny or Beyonce.

Obviously, I don't know him. But my guess would be by 'people like me' he didn't mean white, middle-class men. I suspect that by 'people like me' he simply meant 'me'. He meant 'I can't believe this has happened to me.' Also, there is a type of person like him that something like this doesn't often happen to, and that's someone from a boyband.

Fans have heard Harry say that same line – 'Things like this don't happen to people like me' – many times, at many shows, on, I think, all three tours, so it seemed clear to me that, overwhelmed and thrown by a heckler yelling at him to get off the stage, he reverted to a phrase he's repeated on stage hundreds of times. And while his own fans receive those words in, one assumes, the manner in which he intends them, a wider audience very much did not.

Of course, he may also have been thrown by the technical cock-ups that accompanied his performance of *As It Was*. The spinning stage revolved in the opposite direction, meaning the dancers – and Harry – had to reverse their entire routine, which they had apparently rehearsed for ten days prior to the performance, live.

It's times like these that I feel like I can empathise with Harry the most. In the future, when he looks back on that night, will he remember the achievement? Or will he remember the fuck-ups?

(I once got the opportunity to interview an icon of Young Adult fiction. I was terrified. After the interview, I was massively relieved. I'd got through it! She'd laughed at some of my jokes. I hadn't thrown up or fainted. I was proud of myself. And then she said she appreciated that I'd let her talk so much. Which I interpreted as 'thanks for letting me do all the heavy lifting there. I don't even know why you bothered turning up.')

On winning Best Artist of the Year at the BRITS, less than a week later, Harry ended his (presumably purposefully prepared speech) by saying he is aware of his privilege, before dedicating his award to 'Rina, Charlie, Mabel, Florence, and Becky', some of the women pop stars who missed out after the BRITS made the category gender-neutral, before – disappointingly, but not that surprisingly – nominating an all-male shortlist.

♫ ♫ ♫ ♫ ♫

One of my favourite photos I ever took was after seeing Michael Jackson at Aintree Race Course in September 1988. I don't remember if I took photos during the show, but if I had I can't imagine they were any good, we were so far back. The one photo I have was taken after the show was over, the bright stage lights throwing the leaving fans into silhouettes and revealing the litter-covered ground. The show is over. The music has stopped. The lights are on and we're back in the real world and it's covered with crap.

Where Harry is concerned, I want to live in the show. I don't want the lights on, the stage being dismantled, the staff coming along to tell us we need to leave. I want to stay in the magic. I don't want to be critical. I want unproblematic joy.

Or, as I put it in my group chat, JUST LET ME LOVE ONE SPANGLED MAN.

Chapter Eleven

Fine Line

When I was around 17, my younger sister bought me a jumper. It was cream with a roll neck and bobbles tasselled around the hem. She and her friends declared it the 'most Keris jumper' they'd ever seen. I thanked her, but I was beyond disappointed – I didn't think of myself as a roll neck cream jumper (with bobbles). I didn't know what I was, but I didn't think it was that.

A couple of years later, the Mother I was Helping at my job in London bought me a cardigan. It was expensive (she made a point of telling me), from Monsoon. It was green and patterned, scratchy and uncomfortable. Again, she said she'd bought it because it was so me. I didn't think it was me. I didn't want it to be.

I found this chapter hard to write and for a while, I wasn't sure why. Maybe just because I'm not interested in fashion? Since 2020, I've basically worn a 'uniform' of black stretchy pants and a black V-neck T-shirt. (I have a necklace with an acrylic cut-out of American designer and fashion icon Iris Apfel that I wear for going out.) I love not having to think about clothes or worry about what I'm going to wear to any particular event, but at the same time, I do think I'm missing out.

Coachella sequinned catsuit person is out of my league – I know my limits – but I do think I could be a JW Anderson rainbow patchwork cardigan. Currently, I suspect I'm the Calvin Klein Obsession sweatshirt Harry wore for Radio 1's Big Weekend in 2014 and which, my friends and I joked, had 'day two of period' vibes.

Looking back over photos from the *X Factor* era, no one could ever have imagined that Harry would become the high fashion figure he is today and while of course he didn't do it alone – money and contacts can never be underestimated and nor can being a slender and classically handsome white man – I so admire his style evolution.

From onesies, Uggs, jeans dangling down to show his underwear, he used to dress like the Cheshire teen he was. Obviously, things improved a little with money and fame, but it wasn't until the Gucci floral suits towards the end of One Direction that people really started to take notice.

Since then, his style has continued to evolve. From the flouncy Harris Reed concoctions during his first tour (which Harry described as 'frills and high heels') to the rompers and toddler T-shirts of his stadium tour, he's not afraid of bold colour or pattern and he's not afraid to look daft.

I think one of the (many) appealing things about Harry is how easily he can switch from goofy to sexy and back again and his clothes reflect this. It's unusual for someone considered to be a sex symbol. He clearly doesn't feel the need to be sexy all the time, but nor does he shy away from it. He seems as comfortable on stage dressed not dissimilar to a character from *In the Night Garden* as he does shirtless in leather pants (with the big screen close-ups lingering on his nipples).

When Harry wore a Gucci dress on the cover of *Vogue* in November 2020, right wing commentators were outraged (for a change). Candace Owens tweeted 'Bring back manly men', and Harry uncharacteristically referenced it in an Instagram post, using it as the caption to a photo of him in a pale blue suit, eating a banana.

'I love that how he dresses annoys the sort of people that I want to be annoyed,' my friend Trac commented.

Chloe (of the Harry prints and stickers business) appreciates that Harry, as she puts it, 'maintains his space' in the face of criticism.

'When he did the *Vogue* dress cover shoot the backlash was crazy, but for the most part he didn't acknowledge it. If you're confident within yourself or your work, there's really no need to comment or hit back at anything.'

Vogue wasn't the first time Harry had appeared in a dress and it wouldn't be the last. He's worn a Comme des Garcons pinafore for *The Guardian Weekend* magazine, a pink tutu and tights for *Saturday Night Live* promotional photos, a much-memed green knit number by Jean Paul Gaultier Archive in *Dazed & Confused* magazine, and even appeared on stage dressed as Dorothy from *The Wizard of Oz* for one of his Harryween live shows Madison Square Garden.

Harris Reed, whose designs have been a pivotal part of Harry's fashion evolution and who created the crinoline style dress Harry wore on the inside pages of *Vogue*, told *The Observer* that he wasn't surprised by the backlash, but also, 'how are we still outraged by a man in a dress in 2021?' How indeed.

Unsurprisingly, when Harry wears something by a new designer, it gives them a huge career boost. Harris Reed hadn't yet graduated from Central St Martins when Harry first wore custom Harris Reed – bespoke Italian cream three-tier ruffled blouse and black Venetian wool exaggerated flares with hidden cream Italian silk under flare, still one of my favourite outfits – on stage at Amsterdam's Ziggo Dome.

As a result, Reed told *Harper's Bazaar UK* in 2022, his Instagram followers jumped by 100,000. But more importantly: 'It made my teachers at the time shut up about there being no commerciality in fluidity,' Reed said. 'And it stopped everyone calling me a costume designer or saying I had unrealistic dreams.'

Via his influential stylist Harry Lambert, Harry was Daniel W. Fletcher's first customer, snapping up every short-sleeved shirt from the designer's graduate collection.

'Harry had a huge impact on my career,' Fletcher told *GQ*. 'At 24 years old I couldn't believe what was happening.'

A JW Anderson patchwork cardigan Harry wore for rehearsals for *The Today Show* in 2020 went viral, inspiring myriad replicas and remixes after Anderson made the pattern freely available.

British designer Steven Stokey-Daley had just graduated from Westminster University when he saw an Instagram call-out for emerging designers to submit their work to Harry Lambert for a project he was working on. As a result, Lambert asked Stokey-Daley to send pieces from his graduate collection for the music video for Golden, shot in Portofino, Italy. In the video, Harry wears a white cotton-linen shirt and a pair of floral printed Oxford bags, apparently made from curtains the designer's grandmother found in a charity shop in Liverpool.

'When [the video] came out, he completely widened the spotlight for me,' Stokey-Daley told British *Vogue*. 'There was a huge acceleration in my orders. And it just escalated from there.'

Harry has gone on to become an investor in the SS Daley brand.

In a 2019 article for *The Face*, Elton John compared Harry to Marc Bolan, David Bowie and Mick Jagger, saying 'Harry has the same qualities.'

He does, of course. It was evident from his iconic 2016 shoot for *Another Man*, in which Harry clearly set out to show he wasn't just a boy from a boyband, channelling Bowie and Jagger, along with Paul McCartney (who, in the same issue, gave Harry a masterclass in 'surviving fame, staying grounded and the secret to going solo').

Every now and then, someone will write an article – or a viral tweet – about how Harry's not doing anything new, usually referencing Prince and Bowie, but rarely Little Richard who did it before both of them. But Harry hasn't ever claimed to be doing anything new. He's well aware of his influences (which include Sir Elton John – Harry wore Elton's iconic sparkly Dodgers uniform to a Halloween party in 2018) and he understands fashion.

'There's so much joy to be had in playing with clothes,' Harry told *Vogue*.

Why deny yourself – or anyone else – that joy by sticking to outdated ideas of gendered clothing?

Along with Harry Lambert, Alessandro Michele, former creative director of Gucci, was massively influential in Harry's fashion evolution. First Harry wore the clothes, then he appeared in promotional campaigns (for some reason often cuddling an animal with chickens, goats, lambs and pigs all sharing the shots), and finally revealing his own collection – Gucci Ha Ha Ha – with highlights including a yellow checked suit dotted with cherries, a T-shirt with the brand's sulky teddy logo, and a green checked coat that I could never afford, but which I bookmarked anyway, so I could keep going back to admire it.

Harry's style has been inspiring and freeing for so many fans. I asked a few if Harry has changed the way they dress, starting with one friend who says playing with a version of Harry's look has made her more adventurous in her fashion choices than she might have been before.

> I'm a 50-something woman who doesn't want to wear lots of make up or girly clothes, but neither do I want to go full on butch or completely middle-aged mumsy. I want to be fashionable and trendy. Harry's style is more on the gender neutral spectrum, femme enough to not be butch but with enough masculine energy not to be too femme. This pretty much sums up how I want to present. Pink suits with exaggerated shoulders, huge baby blue fake fur coat, sequinned tops with jeans and colourful trainers. I play with colour and style and get a lot of

> compliments as a result. I've probably moved beyond his aesthetic to something more my own but I know that his influence gave me the confidence to be myself.

Harry's influence giving fans the confidence to be themselves comes up over and over. Laura spent years trying not to be 'too much' until she became a Harry fan:

> I adore Harry's clothing choices for their boldness, colour, camp, fun and all the muchness. I finally realised that you can just be yourself in all that glittery, bold way everyday in every way and that's perfectly fine. Harry can be in plain gym wear or the campest colourful outfit and both are real versions of himself in that moment. Now I dress in a more expressive way and act in a way that is true to myself. Harry's a great example of that for me.

Becky R says seeing Harry embrace his individuality has inspired her to do the same:

> I grew up as the strange or weird kid, and it made me feel ashamed so I would always suppress my interests. There was this one time I wore an outfit that none of my family liked, but I carried on wearing it because if Harry can wear bold fashion choices, get critiqued, yet still carry on – then so can I!

Connor says that what he appreciates is that Harry embraces the culture of 'come as you are'.

> When I was a teenager, I was a fat gay boy who longed to wear sequins and colourful stripes and polka dots, and that seemed impossible to me. I didn't think that was for

> boys, and even if there were some very rare boys who could wear sparkles, those boys couldn't be fat. I grew up before the internet. I grew up before Tumblr. I grew up before Harry Styles. I think he genuinely wants fat people and people in other less socially approved bodies to be his fans. I have no idea what his sexual orientation is, but I just love that he makes me feel special for being gay. He really believes in a sparkly bi aesthetic. And I just adore that.

For Tara Knight, it was the clothes that started it all, she and her daughter, Evalee, were watching a Harry livestream and Evalee asked Tara to make her the pink, sequined fringe vest and wide-leg trousers (which were custom made by Gucci):

> I hadn't used my sewing machine in a very long time but I thought why not, I will give it a go. I made that first outfit and it went from there. I wasn't working and Evalee was only in [kindergarten] two days a week so we would watch the livestream on Instagram and then jump in the car blasting Harry all the way to pick out fabric to make the next outfit. I would make them after each show, sometimes staying up late or getting up very early to finish them. I taught myself how to sew and we would have so much fun filming little videos and dancing around the house in them.

Gucci Ha Ha Ha isn't Harry's only foray into fashion, he also launched beauty brand Pleasing in 2021. Pleasing began with nail varnish and expanded into beauty, clothing and accessories.

I appreciate the diversity of Pleasing's advertising, but I wasn't particularly interested until they announced the fragrances. I'm forever searching for my 'signature scent' and wouldn't it be perfect if

Harry had nailed it for me? I ordered samples of all three fragrances – Rivulets, Bright Hot and Closeness – and crossed my fingers as I tried them. Bright Hot and Closeness unfortunately weren't for me, but Rivulets ('Time suspends, the space remains constant, the center of an old world, new again') smelled so good I had to keep aggressively huffing my own wrist.

Before Pleasing, Harry was one of the faces of Gucci's campaign for Memoire D'une Odeur.

Created by perfumer Alberto Morillas, the literal meaning of the name is 'the memory of a scent', and when I grabbed a sample it immediately brought to mind my nan. I know this sounds like a diss – who wants to smell like a nan? – but it's not. It made me think of Sunday mornings tucked up in my nan's bed with the satin eiderdown and feather mattress with a deep dip in the centre. It smelled like face powder and bed jackets and feeling cosy and safe. The ad campaign uses the Roxy Music song *In Every Dream Home a Heartache*. My nan died in 1986.

I need to check that Celebrity Attitude Scale to see if there's an option for thinking your favourite celebrity is communicating with you via fragrance.

Chapter Twelve

Sparkly bi music

A few years ago, I had a mild Twitter argument with a fellow fan who claimed that in wearing clothing designed for women, Harry wasn't doing anything radical. As I've mentioned, I have two sons. Years ago, on the way home from school one day, the eldest, probably about 4 at the time, told me that his favourite colour used to be pink but it wasn't anymore because pink was 'for girls'. For a while, my youngest had long hair and was constantly mistaken for a girl. Once, choosing glasses at the optician, a member of staff mistook him for a girl and when I corrected him, he said: 'Well his coat doesn't help.' He was wearing a red parka. Red. Not even pink.

My youngest was never bothered about being mistaken for a girl, and once my eldest got a bit older, it didn't bother him either. My point is, just because it doesn't feel radical to you, doesn't mean it's not radical to someone.

Much progress has been made, but gender norms are unfortunately still ingrained, and I love that someone as famous as Harry – and a mainstream teen heartthrob – is out there casually and cheerfully blurring boundaries.

Much of the criticism Harry receives about the clothes he wears is related to his perceived sexuality. He'd be 'allowed' to dress this way if he was openly not straight. He's appropriating queer culture, 'cosplaying as gay', profiting from the queer community while not (openly) being a part of it. This baffles and, honestly, upsets me. Firstly, gender presentation and sexuality are not the same. Secondly, no one has to come out if they don't want to. No one. Harry has stated that he doesn't label his sexuality and yet so many people want to force him to.

Lynsey, who is queer, told me:

> Personally I don't see supporting and affirming queer fans and expressing himself through fashion as appropriation at all. I hugely admire him for not bowing to pressure to define himself in that respect either; and I love how he expresses himself through fashion. I think it's really interesting that people automatically assume he's appropriating queer culture (and often the loudest critics are from within the community, which is so disappointing). Unless he says otherwise, we don't actually know how he identifies, regardless of who he has been involved with.

In a 2022 interview with *Better Homes and Gardens* magazine to promote *Harry's House*, Harry said he's been open with his friends about his sexuality but doesn't feel the need to be public about it, stating 'that's my personal experience; it's mine'.

'I think that, coupled with his attitude towards inclusivity (both verbally and visually), is something that should be recognised and respected,' Lynsey says.

> He doesn't have to do any of that, but he chooses to, which says a lot, I think! Everyone's entitled to privacy and as someone who publicly came out later in life, there are many, many reasons why someone might not want to share. I get really frustrated when people accuse actual human beings living their lives as queerbaiting; as a performer, the focus should be on his music and performance, not us feeling entitled to every detail of his life.

'Harry's never pretended to be gay and hasn't hidden the fact that he's been romantically linked with lots of good-looking women,' Connor agrees. 'There are some implications of bisexuality in some of his songs and some of his knowing comments – most recently referring to his whole concert as "sparkly bi music".'

Lynsey referenced the 'sparkly bi music' comment too. Harry said it on stage at Wembley in June 2023 – I was there, it was the last time I saw him live. Helping a fan come out, Harry asked what kind of music they wanted the band to play. When the fan asked for 'sparkly bi music', Harry said, 'Is not all of this sparkly bi music?' It made me laugh, but yes, like Lynsey says, it made me feel affirmed. It made me feel, again, that I was in the right place with the right person.

'He might be straight, but if he is, he's a straight man who wraps himself in our flag and who sings our songs,' Connor says.

> He's a man who inserted YMCA into the bridge into *Music From a Sushi Restaurant* in his Love on Tour set, he's a man who wears glitter and sparkles and feather boas and he's a man who helps a young person come out at every other concert he does. And even if he is 100 per cent straight (and who really is?), I don't think he goes home and curses the gays and hates the sparkle and burns rainbow flags while counting our money. I think he loves the rainbows and the sparkles and the bisexual music.

I think so too. And even if Harry is straight, then, as Louis Staples wrote in *The Face* magazine: 'If gender is a construct, with visual and sexual norms that restrict how many of us live our lives, then why should Styles be excluded from its abolition?'

Asked about Harry's *Vogue* cover, the gender non-conforming writer and performance artist Alok Vaid-Menon said they want a world where everyone, regardless of gender, can wear whatever they want. '[Harry] is exercising that and giving permission for other people to do the same and that makes me so happy! I can both celebrate that and be cautious about the politics of representation.'

It's possible to praise Harry for this while also pointing out that trans women and femmes don't get a platform to do what Harry is doing and are at risk of being harassed or even killed for doing it.

'Harry's fashion style is undoubtedly queer-coded and blurs gender lines,' Jen Wilde wrote on her Substack. But, she says, because he hasn't had a 'coming out' moment, where he's declared in clear terms that he is bisexual/pansexual/queer, then he is assumed to be straight and therefore 'committing the crime of queerbaiting for profit'.

The message this sends, Jen says, is that before you do or say anything that could be interpreted as queer, you must first announce your sexuality publicly.

Many fans believe that Harry has announced his sexuality publicly. In 2014, during an interview to promote One Direction's fourth album, *Four*, Harry and Liam were asked what traits they look for in a girl?

'Female,' Liam answered. 'That's a good trait.'

And Harry shrugged and said, 'Not that important.'

A mainstream popstar whose early persona was built around him being a womaniser clearly stating that gender is not a consideration in who he would choose to date – instead he suggested 'sense of humour' and 'being nice to people' as the traits he admired – felt pretty radical then and while it's not exactly a coming out, it's not nothing.

'I think we go to a strange place when we talk about queerbaiting in the context of real people,' Michael says.

> I get it, but queerness is a lot of things – it's a broad church and it's a lived experience, it's a way of moving through the world – and these conversations about queerbaiting reduce it down to a sequinned jacket or a bloke painting

> his nails. I just find it reductive and unhelpful. I find the whole conversation quite distasteful.
>
> For me, I think the more helpful way of framing stuff is about exploitation, and if I thought Harry was exploiting his queer fans I would have something to say, I wouldn't support that. But I don't think he is, I think he's celebrating and affirming them, I think that's powerful, I think that's good.

'This entitlement, this binary view of out/straight leaves no room for fluidity or privacy,' Jen writes. 'How does this look to someone who is still figuring themselves out? What if you don't like labels? What if you need time to explore who you are? What if, god forbid, you just want to keep some things for yourself?'

As someone who didn't realise or accept my own sexuality until well into my forties, I can tell you how it feels. It feels like shit. And it feels even shittier when it comes from within the LGBT+ community. Harry Styles won't see your hot takes about how there's literally no reason for him not to come out, but your friends who are still unsure of or uncomfortable with their sexuality will.

When I was a teenager, I read an article in a magazine about sexuality and the writer said that fantasising about women doesn't mean you're a lesbian. I remember thinking 'Oh thank god.' This was the eighties. The first time I heard the word lesbian was a schoolfriend calling two girls 'lezzers' for hugging or holding hands or something equally innocuous. As far as I was concerned, there were no lesbians on TV (until Ellen came out in 1994, the year Harry Styles was born).

I didn't have a boyfriend in my teens. I remember my mum once asking me if I was gay and I said absolutely not. My sister told me recently that she and Mum had discussed it – discussed me – too. I had no idea. My teens were almost entirely dedicated to being a fan. To yearning. To dreaming about the future, somewhere else (London) where I could be a different person. Or rather, the person I thought I already was but couldn't be at home on the Wirral.

There's an episode of *The Simpsons* where Lisa is reading a magazine called *Non-Threatening Boys*. I still think about it often, because that was my teens. I put all my time and energy, romantic and sexual interest into the people in posters on my bedroom wall. From John Travolta to Bucks Fizz (I kissed a photo of Mike Nolan every night until his lips had literally worn away, revealing the white paper beneath) to Paul Young, Nik Kershaw, Wham!, Terence Trent D'Arby, and then Bros.

I finally got myself a boyfriend in my early twenties. And we got married a couple of years later, also in my early twenties.

A few years ago, a lesbian friend held her arm out and asked me if 100 per cent straight was at the fingertips and 100 per cent gay was the elbow, where would I put myself? The first time she asked, I got all flustered thinking did it have to be stuff I'd done or could it just be what I'd thought about? What were the parameters? I needed more information! When she asked me again the following year (we only ever saw each other at a convention), I'd had time to ponder it and I felt like I was probably closer to the elbow than the fingertips.

I think as a teen I was worried about being gay – and to be honest, probably later in life too – and would think 'oh I'm definitely attracted to men so not gay, phew', but for some reason never actually considered that I might be bi. Once I realised or accepted it was an option, it seemed really obvious.

I got to know Martina first through the Slack and in 2018, she direct messaged me to ask me about my later in life bi realisation, which I'd talked about online (because I talk about everything online) and I subsequently became the first person she came out to.

'I guess for me it was the first time that a big part of my life (because the fandom at that time was a huge part of my life!) wasn't heteronormative,' Martina told me.

> Which meant that I was 'allowed', and able, to see myself and my experiences through a new, or rather, a more open/broad lens. Like, 'Ohhhhh yeah when I watch the female footy players, I'm enjoying it because they're hot. They make me feel things. It's not because I've suddenly developed a love for footy.' And then when you shared your experience, that opened the door even further. Because suddenly – not everyone realises they're bisexual when they're young? Being married doesn't have to mean I'm straight??

Brigid's experience was similar.

> Growing up a female Gen Xer, unless you were very definitely a lesbian, you could pretty much just believe you liked a woman because you wanted to be her (not be with her),' she told me. 'My mum did ask me if I was a lesbian when I was about 15, but I think that was because at the time I had short hair and lived in jeans.

For many fans, Harry – and, earlier, One Direction – has provided a safe space to explore their sexual identity.

'Before I fell down the One Direction rabbit hole I didn't know I was queer,' Brigid said.

> I knew that my sexuality wasn't quite the same as everyone else's and had dabbled in some BDSM (lite) relationships to see if that was the issue but that didn't fit either.
>
> However once in the fandom my mind was opened to so many different identities that I hadn't realised existed or hadn't appreciated. Like I didn't really understand asexuality, but when I realised it wasn't that you didn't

> like sex but was that you just didn't have primary sexual attraction it was like a door opened. Then through reading fan fiction, I became more certain I was queer. Harry and the boys were the canvases upon which queer people could explore parts of themselves that they didn't understand.
>
> Harry in particular resonated as someone who was performing straightness the same way I did, able to pass successfully but signalling something else. Is this me projecting? Maybe, but he is the person who seemed to make sense. Is he the whole reason I figured out I was queer? No. But if it hadn't been for the One Direction fandom and then latterly his solo career, I'd probably be trying to make a heterosexual relationship work and have no idea why I was miserable.

In 2018, my friend Kat took an ace flag to her Harry show, the first time she'd taken any flag to any show:

> That the flag was an ace flag was just something that I could never have imagined being brave enough to do. I had accepted my bisexuality for decades, but hadn't been honest with myself that my queerness had changed and that I wasn't happy.
>
> Harry's first tour started in September 2017 and I went to several shows. I kept seeing everyone with their Pride flags. Lesbian Pride flags and trans Pride flags. At the DC show, there was a young person with a nonbinary flag and I asked them about it and they told me all about it. I got home from that show and looked online and found a site explaining everything about sexuality and sexual identity and I read about asexuality, aromanticism and I ordered an ace flag right then and there.

> In June 2018, I went to another show and I'd arranged to meet a group of queer women and nonbinary people. Total strangers. I showed up with my ace flag and I felt comfortable in my skin for the first time in a really long time. I had my flag folded in my bag. In the venue, no one around me had flags and I felt a little uncomfortable. But then Harry did his usual 'safe space' announcement and I took out my flag and shook it free and I held it throughout the entire concert.
>
> I had come out as bi in my twenties so it wasn't as if I was in the closet and I had been comfortable for decades in that truth, but I'd been denying how my queerness had changed and evolved and Harry made me feel like it was okay to be completely honest with myself and others.

Fan fiction also led Kat to a better understanding of her sexuality:

> When I joined the Slack, it exposed me to more One Direction fan fiction and that was important because all of a sudden I was finding fics that featured demisexual and asexual characters. I knew what the definition of a demisexual and asexual person was, but I'd never really read anything where a character was asexual and here I was reading fanfiction that was so well-written. These characters were expressing feelings that I'd felt for years but had pushed deep down, hiding it and ignoring it. My last serious relationship, one of the main reasons it finally ended was because I just didn't care about sex anymore. And I didn't know how to express it. Two years later I'm reading this silly fan fiction and there was a Harry character telling another character exactly what they were and why they were asexual and why it was important and all about aromanticism and all these things that I felt deep down.

Harry has always had a strong queer fandom and I'm often surprised when people are surprised by that. I remember a tweet asking how and why Harry could possibly be a 'lesbian icon' and yet there's a long history of gay men having female icons, from Liza Minelli to Cher to Kylie Minogue.

'I think his popularity with queer fans goes beyond the flag waving (which I love!) and the ostentatious outfits (also a fan!) in a way that it's really hard to put your finger on,' Michael says.

> For me, he treads this really fine line between being engaged and not overstepping the mark: he's been a vocal ally and very supportive of queer and trans fans – he's actively celebrated queer and trans fans in his shows, there are some really moving videos of him helping gay and trans fans come out during his gigs – at a time when making those kind of public declarations can be hard.
>
> There's something incredibly heart-warming and affirming about Harry – huge, world-beating, popstar Harry – saying this is cool, this is alright, this is a space and a place you're welcome in and, look, everybody agrees.
>
> At the same time, he hasn't engaged with political conversations that I don't necessarily think are his place to engage with, and I'm happy about that. I think a lot of popstars and celebrities are treading on toes by flying into conversations they have no context for, saying things that aren't helpful or useful, and sometimes doing more damage than good.

At one of his earliest solo shows, Harry announced, 'If you are Black, if you are white, if you are gay, if you are straight, if you are transgender — whoever you are, whoever you want to be, I support you. I love every single one of you.'

The fans unsurprisingly took this to heart and Harry ended up helping someone come out at practically every show.

The most infamous occasion became a meme along the lines of 'Harold, they're lesbians' (about the film *Carol* and unrelated to Mr Styles). At her eighth show in San Jose, California, a fan named Grace made a sign that read, 'I'm going to come out to my parents because of you.' Of course Harry spotted it. 'He first asked if he could read the sign out loud, which I thought was very thoughtful and polite,' Grace told Buzzfeed. He then asked for Grace's mum's name and when Grace told him it was Tina and that she was in a hotel room a few miles away, Harry shushed the crowd before yelling, 'TINA, SHE'S GAY!' It brought the house down.

Afterwards, on Instagram, Grace posted, 'Thank you so much for creating an environment where I am proud to be who I am. Your continuous support of the LGBTQ+ [community] has helped me come to love myself and feel safe.'

It's one of author Jen Wilde's favourite things too:

> There are so many videos online of these moments that are just so wholesome, joyful, and celebratory, with crowds cheering as one person comes out. Knowing a whole stadium of people – including your musical icon – are celebrating your queerness? Growing up, I couldn't have imagined something like that ever being real.

On a podcast a couple of years ago, I heard the singer Brandi Carlisle say that she's sometimes envious of people who came out later in life because they 'missed so much shit,' but that maybe coming out earlier is better. To get it over with. 'Like chickenpox.'

She joked that you could have chickenpox parties for queerness. And I immediately thought, that's a Harry Styles show.

Chapter Thirteen

Adore You

I love an origin story. When I meet a Harry fan, one of the first things I ask is how they fell for him. The stories are often similar but also frequently personal.

'Do you remember that Tumblr post?' my friend Lindsay said when I asked her. 'It was something like "Day One: I'll just look up what the curly one is called? Two Weeks Later: That's not Harry, he doesn't breathe like that." It was exactly like that.'

I do remember that post. And also a gif from a One Direction gig that shows Harry reaching up through the trap door in the stage to grab Niall by his vest and pull him down too. That's how it happens. Harry reaches up and pulls you in and down the rabbit hole you go.

When I spoke to fans for this book, I asked what they'd ask other fans and many of them said they'd ask how it happened for them. So then I asked everyone.

Michael Lee Richardson, 37 but I tell people I'm 35, Glasgow, working class, they/them.

> Harry was always my favourite – he's got such a brilliant pop voice, not the best singer in that group but, I think, the most recognisable. I think he really influenced One Direction's sound, especially later on. I actually still remember watching that first audition, that VT beforehand, where he talked about working in a bakery and being in a band, and then he came onstage with that silly hair, in that

ridiculous scarf, and just had the most gorgeous voice – I think you can really see, even that early, what he was and what he'd become. There's just something so likeable about him, and there's such a purity to it.

I loved One Direction – *Made in the AM* is always in my most played, especially *If I Could Fly* – but it was when Harry went solo that it really, really clicked, for me. Hearing *Sign of the Times* and watching that video for the first time, it was just like, 'oh, there he is' – the popstar I could always see he'd become, and there it was.

Author Jen Wilde. 36. Brooklyn, NY.

I had been hired by Wattpad and Sony Pictures to write a serial fiction story to promote the film *Pride and Prejudice and Zombies*. The story had to combine zombies with the popular Wattpad book *After by Anna Todd* (weird combo, I know!). *After* began as One Direction/Harry Styles fanfiction, so I watched some One Direction music videos and Late Show interviews. The more I watched, the more I started to get why they were so popular. By the time I'd finished the writing project, I was obsessed. Harry was instantly my favourite. My timing wasn't so great though: the band did their final performance together that same week.

Liz Harvatine, 43, Burbank, CA

Being pregnant and parenting babies was really hard for me mentally and the difficulties (obviously) compounded with each kid. When my youngest was almost 2, coming out of babyhood, I started to feel a little space opening up that might allow me to find some of myself again. I used to read all the time but had barely read anything in the six years I'd been a parent. I made an effort to get into books again.

One of the books I read in those first few months of being back at it was *Carry On*, by Rainbow Rowell. I became obsessed with the book in a way I hadn't been obsessed with anything in years. I was beyond thrilled the following year, when Rainbow announced there would be a sequel to *Carry On*. She announced the book with an image of the two main characters, one, named Baz, was wearing an eye-catching, colourful floral suit. Wading through all the excited chatter on social media, I kept seeing fans leave the same comment: Baz looks like Harry! So many of Rainbow's readers and lovers of *Carry On* were also Harry Styles fans. I barely knew who he was at that point but this planted a little Harry seed in my head.

It was a month or two later when I was feeling pretty depressed and that seed grew into the impulse to watch some videos of him on YouTube. I think I spent an entire afternoon doing this and I'm not talking about music videos or performances, I'm talking everything but. Interviews and late night appearances and (imo) the Rosetta Stone of early solo career Harry, the ultimate showcase of his charm and humour with just enough musical performance to complete the package, guaranteed to induce obsession: Carpool Karaoke. That was that. I fell down the Harry hole and I've never come back.

Connor, 42-year-old Irish gay man, living in London.

In 2010, I started spending a lot of time on YouTube. People who have never followed YouTubers will never know what it's like to start following someone on YouTube for years on end until you feel you're enmeshed in their lives and they genuinely begin to feel like your friends.

At that stage, I'd been single all my life (other than a brief and glorious ten-day fling when I was 26), and it didn't seem as if that was going to change any time soon. I had lots of close female friends, but very few male friends, and I'd begun to believe that men just didn't like me. When I did make male friendships, they often burned out quickly. The people on YouTube were different. They were safe.

I found myself getting very invested in the lives of YouTubers like Dan and Phil, and I also found myself watching videos of One Direction interviews over and over again. There were the famous interviews they did on the stairs during *X Factor*, the cooking videos, the quizzes, all part of the backstage promotion for the show. I watched these videos and fell in love with the relationship these boys had with each other. This was safe male friendship. These boys weren't going to reject me. And there was so much content out there.

I remember one video especially that I used to watch all of the time, but seems to have been taken down. It was a video of Harry meeting fans, who would be crying and emotional because they were meeting One Direction, and Harry would say 'Are you OK?' and hug them, and I'd watch that video over and over and it would soothe me. I think a lot of my friends thought there was something sordid about me liking One Direction, given that I'm about twelve years older than them, but I genuinely just wanted to be their friend. I just wanted Harry to ask me if I was OK.

Lindsay, 45, Newcastle

The first time I saw Harry was on *The X Factor* when he was put into One Direction. I thought he looked cute but I didn't fit their target audience and so didn't pay much attention. I was teaching when 1D mania started and I can remember having a couple of lessons disrupted as girls in my class were checking their phones for a tour announcement. I had to work hard to transport myself back to their age and being obsessed with Bros to understand why they were shrieking and making such a fuss. When I dug deep though, I got it. I remembered that feeling.

I became a Harry fan when my small children came home from school singing 1D songs. Their teacher was using *Live While We're Young* as their Wake Up Shake Up song so we found the video on YouTube for them to watch at home. And then we watched another … and another … and another … until the children had wandered off to play and it was just me watching on my own.

Amy Miller, 37-year-old mum from Los Angeles

I was doing another event in the Staples Center at the same time as One Direction's show and while going into the building to find a restroom, I happened to run into all the boys and their security as they shuffled them single file down a corridor.

Harry, in his very Harry way, stopped me and asked if I was going to the show. I eloquently told him I had to pee. After telling me several times I should check out the show (as if it hadn't been sold out for ages) and being told off by Niall to leave me alone so I could use the toilet, he scampered off with that cheeky little smile on his face knowing he had just snagged another soul. And obviously, as soon as my event was over, I dragged my friend to the box office to see if by chance there were any nosebleeds or will calls not picked up left that we could purchase.

Our last dollars and some haggling/begging later, we ran to the tippy top row twenty minutes into the show and the rest is history.

Kat, 52 – lives in Seattle, WA

My friend Dave used to live next to the Manhattan hotel where *Saturday Night Live* put up most of their guests and music acts. I was visiting one weekend and Saturday morning we could hear the sounds of girls singing below. Dave and I enjoyed our coffee as we leaned out the window and watched about fifty young women standing and sitting on the sidewalk outside of the hotel. We didn't recognise anything the girls were singing and after a bit we went on with our day.

Later that evening when we got home from seeing a play, Dave suggested we watch *SNL* to see the musical guest that had all those girls so excited. One Direction. I was mesmerised by those five young guys. So cute. Wearing full on suits with vests and suspenders and shit. Harry was wearing a bowtie. I knew that if these five people had been around when I was 15? It would've been all over for my heart. I would've been done for.

I hadn't had a true fandom experience as a teenager. Sure, I was obsessed with Duran Duran, but I didn't follow everything they did. I was a part of the Washington DC punk and hardcore scene, but for me that was more about wanting to date the guys in the band, more than the music. I didn't really like most of the music I was listening to because I was just listening to be 'cool'. I found One Direction's brand of pop music to be delightful and I started to listen to it a lot, especially in my car.

Before Harry Styles I would've said that I didn't have a maternal bone in my body. I was endlessly endeared by Harry. It was undeniable. That sense of protectiveness extended into 2017 when Harry's solo career was beginning. The lead up to Harry releasing his first solo album was insane. The first *Rolling Stone* cover and article; the incredible *Another Man* photo shoots; the Apple documentary *Behind the Album*. By the time summer 2017 had rolled around and Harry was about to begin his first ever solo tour, I was fully invested and obsessed with him. My obsession and love has only grown from there.

Kimberley, 50, DC, psychotherapist and author

Harry kept popping up in Instagram and I asked my partner, 'Why is Harry Styles all over my feed? I don't even know him!' My partner replied that women of a certain age really liked him. This was around the time of his sold-out NYC shows and the *Vogue* article 'Why do women in their 40s love Harry Styles so much', and I begin to pay attention.

I watched some Reels, wasn't impressed with the little bit of music I heard and moved along. Then I listened to all his music on Spotify during a two-hour drive and became enamoured. Like really enamoured. When I got to my destination, I texted my partner and said, 'I think I have a crush on Harry Styles'. My days started with watching more and more of his Reels and I booked a flight, hotel, and ticket to his Chicago show solo.

After sharing my new passion for him on Instagram, someone told me to read *The Idea of You*. I don't typically read fiction, but I trusted her judgment and devoured it in one night. For weeks I woke up with a pep in my step and then booked tickets to see him in Paris the following June. Both nights.

Martina, 42, Australia

I was in the car, driving to work. There was traffic, and I was flicking through commercial radio stations (which I never listened to, as I was a proper music snob), trying to find a traffic report. I heard part of a song, liked it, Shazamed it, and was shocked. *Sign of the Times* by Harry Styles. Harry Styles? Isn't he from that boyband? Like ten minutes later, the same thing happened on a different radio station with another H song (*Sweet Creature* this time). That was the beginning of it all for me.

I tried to pretend none of that had happened, but I'd just really liked both songs, so ended up listening to them on YouTube. But there was no way it was going to get any bigger than that, no siree.

I think the album had been released for all of a week when I gave into my curiosity and listened to the whole thing. I fell in love with it instantly, and with him gradually over the next couple of weeks as I delved into general 1D fandom.

Lexy Jones, 21, graphic artist, social media content creator, and small business owner from South Carolina. Senior at Clemson University studying Graphic Communications

What Makes You Beautiful was released when I was around 9 years old, and I quickly became infatuated with One Direction. When I was 15, Harry released *Sign of the*

Times. I remember one of my teachers playing it in our classroom and later that day I downloaded it and listened to it on repeat for a week straight.

Now that I was old enough to stream my own music, I was so excited for the rest of the album to come out. I was never a full album listener until then, but Harry's first album changed everything for me, and I have never listened to music in the same way again. I fell in love with his album, watched so many interviews like his Carpool Karaoke and *Behind the Album* documentary and fell in love with his personality too.

I knew I had a new lifelong favourite musician.

Chapter Fourteen

Girl Crush

'I'm not even the main character of my own life, Harry Styles is.'

I love this much-memed quote and it made me laugh so much when I first read it, but it's not true (although it's not *not* true).

Harry has been, for me, more like a Manic Pixie Dreamgirl. Film critic Nathan Rabin, who coined the term (and, yes, has since disavowed it as sexist) said that the Manic Pixie Dreamgirl 'exists solely in the fevered imaginations of sensitive writer-directors to teach broodingly soulful young men to embrace life and its infinite mysteries and adventures'.

While Harry Styles the person obviously doesn't exist solely in anyone's fevered imaginations, his persona, the pop star, the celebrity, certainly does. And he – along with the friends I made through his fandom – very much taught me or reminded me how to embrace life and adventure.

In early 2024, I finally made the pilgrimage to Holmes Chapel to see Harry Styles's actual house… that he hasn't lived in since 2010 when he beetled off to London, aged 16, to audition for X Factor – and never went home.

I'd often joked about going there, but never really felt the need, but then I read about a Harry walking tour and map created by the Holmes Chapel Partnership and I figured it was time for me to go. You know, for research. And I took my sister along too. Because she, unlike me, has a car.

Our first stop was of course W. Mandeville, the bakery where teen Harry had a Saturday job. My sister bought cheese. I bought apple slices to take home for my kids. Perfectly reasonable reasons to be in there, but I felt self-conscious, like I had a flashing sign over my head that said I AM HERE BECAUSE OF HARRY STYLES.

While we were paying, another customer came in, another middle-aged woman, and she instantly snapped a photo of the Harry poster before placing her own order. Maybe everyone was there for Harry Styles.

Until I read about the tour, I hadn't known about the Harry wall at the viaduct. I've watched the One Direction documentary This Is Us (more than once), I've seen Harry talking about the wall where he wrote his name (and possibly had his first kiss), but I didn't know fans had turned it into a shrine … And this was partly the reason the map was produced, to suggest a safer route to the viaduct.

According to the Holmes Chapel Partnership, 'These fans risk life and limb walking down the A535 on a narrow, overgrown footpath to cross the road and climb over a stile with a steep drop on the other side.'

We definitely didn't want to do that. We looked at the map. We couldn't work out the route. I searched the viaduct on Google Maps … and off we went, risking life and limb by walking down the A535.

We found the viaduct. As we approached, I skidded in the mud, windmilling my arms just as my sister turned back to check on me. She laughed, as did the only other fans we saw all day (as far as we know, anyway). Rude.

We were at the wrong bit of the viaduct, which the other fans worked out before we did (but didn't tell us; so much for treating people with kindness!). But a bit further along the death-trap A535, over Harry's stile, down the steep drop (I slipped in the mud again), we finally found it and it was actually really lovely, covered with quotes from songs and interviews, fandom in jokes, telephone numbers and bold declarations ('I AM GAY').

A pilgrimage, Lucy James writes in her dissertation, is not necessarily about the actual visit, but what is experienced personally during or after the visit. I feel like this is something I've always tried to explain to people about fandom. It's not just the thing. It's how you feel about the thing.

I would never have waited outside Matt Goss's house for five thousand hours alone. Even back then, when people asked me what on earth I was doing, I told them it wasn't about him. Not really. It was about being with my friends. The laughter. The in-jokes. The shared experience.

I'm still friends with many of the women I met outside Matt Goss's apartment. I asked if they remember why we did it.

'It was the feeling you were sharing something with them that most fans could only dream of,' Suzi said. 'I remember telling my friends at school and everyone being so jealous. Also, most of the other fans outside became friends. It was a feeling of being part of a community.'

It's always about the community.

And community, Psychologist Erin le Clerc tells me, 'encourages us to grow, to find our voice, to feel confident, and to become a part of something that feels purposeful to us, which can result in improved mood, reduced anxiety, and a greater sense of quality of life.'

'To actually just be able to lean into that feminine communion,' Tabitha Carvan says, 'something that has been disparaged and embarrassing and cringeworthy for so long. I think the scale on which Harry has done that is amazing.'

In the documentary about the movie Greatest Days, my old nemesis, Gary Barlow, talks about how Take That fans meet each other through the band and then get together for the shows, having parties, hanging out the night before.

'We're just part of the activities,' he says. 'We're not all of it.'

The friends I met through Harry have become some of my closest. We talk pretty much every day. We've been on (Harry-centred) holidays together. They're often the first people I talk to in the morning and the last people I talk to at night. (Yes, pretty much all of this talking is done online, but that makes no difference to me.) They know pretty much everything about my life.

Jen Wilde says Harry has helped her make friends:

> Finding queer women my age online who are big Harry fans has been so rewarding. His music helped me process my emotions as I fell in love during the pandemic, and watching him step into himself over the years gave me the extra confidence I needed to do the same.

'Being a Harry fan is almost like a secret club,' Laura says. 'When you know someone is a fan then it's like unlocking an instant bond.'

I met one of the friends I went to Los Angeles with in 2018 when she turned up at an author event in a local bookshop, wearing a Harry T-shirt. As soon as I saw her, my brain went 'Friend!' and I couldn't wait to talk to her. One month later, we were in LA together for the final shows of the tour.

I'd known Alicia through Twitter for years and then we moved our almost daily Harry chat to WhatsApp, along with a few other Twitter friends. In New York to see Harry in 2018, seven of us had lunch with the final member of the group FaceTiming in from Malaysia.

'I think the relationships I've made through his fandom have made me more open and confident,' Alicia says. 'More like myself.'

The same for me. Absolutely. Being able to shout about what you love and have friends who not only understand but will happily shout back cannot be underestimated.

'I belong to this fandom with people from across the generations,' Michael says, 'people of all genders and sexual orientations, people of all races and religions, but we've all got something in common because we're just really, really into this one (incredibly hot) guy and his music, and I think that's beautiful.'

♫ ♫ ♫ ♫ ♫

'People don't come to see me be me,' Dolly Parton said in a 2020 interview, 'but, instead, come to see me be them.'

I look at that photo I took of myself in Paris and it feels like me. Running down the steps in New York with my Metrocard feels like me. On the subway platform with my wet hair and earbuds feels like me. Struggling to sing *Tiny Dancer* (enunciate, Elton!) with my friends as we drove across Australia feels like me. Crying at *Lights Up* feels like me. Trying (and failing) to do the boot scoot feels like me. Watching a heart-shaped balloon float away against a cornflower sky feels like me. Taking off my bra and then having to hold a boob in each hand to dance feels like me.

Writing this book has been a fascinating experience. I've managed to piece and link together so many parts of myself that I previously considered entirely unrelated.

Writing this book has felt like me.

In *Arrangements in Blue*, poet Amy Key's memoir of a life without romantic love and how Joni Mitchell's *Blue* shaped her, she writes about watching Peter Jackson's eight-hour Beatles documentary, *Get Back*, and how John Lennon asks Ringo Starr to cue his vocal with a cymbal, to give him 'the courage to come screaming in'. Amy writes that she was moved by John needing encouragement from his friend 'to not only enter, but to enter the song with terrific power'. She writes: 'So many things have the power to make us the version of ourselves we long for. To step beyond what we thought we were.'

Harry gave me the power to get back to where I once belonged. Not only in a physical sense – returning to the town I grew up in – but also in returning to fandom. And remembering the girl I used to be encouraged me to move forward. To step into the light.

Lights Up may be my favourite Harry song, but I always struggled with the repeated refrain 'Do you know who you are?' Because I didn't. But I wanted to. I wanted to try to find out, work it out. And I think maybe I finally have.

I'm someone who, when I love something, I am all in. The things I love, I love excessively. I am happy to make them my entire personality. But I also want to share them with friends, with people who understand. And even with people who don't, because maybe if I can make them understand, they can share some of the joy.

I always want to share the joy.

In *This Is What It Sounds Like*, Susan Rogers writes, 'Be it records or romantic partners, we fall in love with the ones who make us feel like our best and truest self.'

Harry – and my fandom friends (who I usually just call my friends) – make me feel like my best and truest self. This is me, sharing the joy.

Bibliography

Books

Ashley, B. (2020) *Gold light shining* Banshee Press

Bateman, J. (2018) *Fame: The Hijacking of Reality* Akashic Books, US

Carvan, T. (2022) *This Is Not a Book About Benedict Cumberbatch* HarperCollins Australia

Cashmore, E. (2023) *Celebrity Culture* Routledge; 3rd edition

Clarke, C. (2019) *The Pants Project* Sourcebooks Young Readers

Dederer, C. (2023) *Monsters: A Fan's Dilemma* Sceptre

Edelman, H. (1994) *Motherless Daughters* Da Capo Lifelong Books

Heath, C. (2004) *Feel* Ebury Press

Heath, C. (2017) *Reveal* Blink Publishing

Heisey, M. (2023) *Really Good, Actually: A Novel.* Fourth Estate

Jong, E. (1973) *Fear of Flying* Holt, Rinehart and Winston, US

Lee, R. (2017) *The Idea of You* Penguin

Lundin, B. (2018) *Ship It* Freeform, US

Manning, S. (2023) *The Man of Her Dreams* Hodder & Stoughton

Manning, S. (2014) *The Worst Girlfriend In The World* Atom

Melnick, L (2022) I've Had to Think Up a Way to Survive, University of Texas Press.

Rogers, S. and Ogas, O. (2022) *This Is What It Sounds Like* Vintage Digital

Spears, B. (2023) *The Woman in Me* Gallery UK

Stainton, K. (2017) *It Had to be You* Bookouture

Stainton, K. (2017) *One Italian Summer* Hot Key Books

Stainton, K. (2018) *My Heart Goes Bang* Hot Key Books
Tandoh, R. (2016) *Flavour: Eat What You Love* Chatto & Windus

Podcasts

Griefcast, Ep.76 Felix White, 17 April 2019
Weirdos Book Club, Ep. 12 Y/N by Esther Yi, 9 November 2023
Weirdos Book Club, Ep. 2 Really Good, Actually by Monica Heisey with Monica Heisey, 31 August 2023
Justin Hawkins Rides Again, Ep. 33 Does Fandom Ever Go Too Far, 23 January 2024
We Can Do Hard Things, Ep. 253 Is it Real Love or Spider Love with Martha Beck, 26 October 2023
Speaks Volumes with Derrick Gee, Ep. 59 Harry Styles' Creative Director Molly Hawkins on Empathy, World Building, and Putting the Artist First, 12 June 2024

Documentaries

Take That's Greatest Days: 30 Years in the Making, RWD Films, 2023
One Direction – A Year in the Making, TV movie 2011 dir. Ben Winston
Harry Styles: Behind the Album – Apple TV, 2017 dir. Paul Dugdale
One Direction: This Is Us, 2013 dir. Morgan Spurlock
Robbie Williams, 2023 dir. Joe Pearlman
Harry's House – Zane Lowe, Apple Music, 2019
The Making of a Boyband, BBC, 1993

Films

Greatest Days (2023): Elysian Film Group

Magazine Articles

Spanos, B. (2022) 'How Harry Styles Became the World's Most Wanted Man', *Rolling Stone*, August.

Crowe, C. (2017) 'Harry Styles' New Direction', *Rolling Stone*, April.

Styles, G. (2016) 'Gemma Styles on Growing Up With Her Brother', *Another Man*, A/W 2016.

Doyle, P. (2015) '5 Seconds of Summer: Inside the Wild Life of the World's Hottest Band', *Rolling Stone*, December.

Stoppard, L. (2022) 'Finding Home: Harry Styles Reveals the Meaning Behind His New Album, "Harry's House"', *Better Homes & Gardens*, April.

Lamont, T (2019) 'I'm not just sprinkling in sexual ambiguity to be interesting', *Guardian Weekend*, December.

Bowles, H. (2020) 'Playtime With Harry Styles', *Vogue*, November.

Newspaper Article

Bradley, F. (2024) 'Why some fans boo Taylor Swift at Travis Kelce's games: the "Anti-Hero" superstar might be loved by Swifties, but the hardcore, sport-loving "Brads and Chads" don't like the shifted attention', *South China Morning Post*, February.

Lindquist, D. (2018) '5 ways Harry Styles charted his own course in Indianapolis', Indianapolis Star

Online Essays

Romanoff, Z. (2018) 'We (Self) Care Too Much ', Substack. *Two Bossy Dames*, 13 April.

Brookover, S. (2018) 'I Stan A Legend of The Joyful Jet Engine', Substack. *Two Bossy Dames*, 23 June.

Lansom, A. (2023) 'Misogyny Towards Fandoms & Fangirls Is Still A Problem ', *Refinery29*, 26 July.

Khan, A (2018) 'Harry Styles' Show Was The Best Queer Girl's Pride Celebration Ever', *Them*, 25 June.

Marlowe, G (2022) 'Treat People With Kindness: The story behind the song', *Medium*, 3 July.

Howell, S (2019) 'Patron Saint of My Teens', *Kill Your Darlings*, 26 August.

Abdurraqib , H (2017) 'Aging Out of Diehard Fandom Is Bittersweet', *Buzzfeed News*, 18 September.

Petersen, A. (2022) 'Who Gets "Quality" Leisure?', Substack. Culture Study, 20 November.

DiBenedetto, C. & Cavender E. (2023) 'You're not getting old, concerts are weird now', Mashable, 27 January 2023.

Online Presentations

Everything Breaks at Scale – Sacha Judd, Beyond Tellerrand in May 2022

For the Love of Fangirls – Yve Blake, TED, 2019

Academic Articles

Ehrenreich, B, Hess, E. and Jacobs, G. (1992), 'Girls Just Want to Have Fun'

Dunn, C. (2012) 'The female fan's relationship with the figure of the male footballer and her favourite players' (not included in PhD thesis)

Mikel Brown, L. and Gilligan, C. (1993), 'Meeting at the Crossroads: Women's Psychology and Girls' Development'

Anderson, T. (2012), 'Still Kissing Their Posters Goodnight: Lifelong Pop Music Fandom', Doctoral thesis, University of Sunderland

James, L. (2022/23), 'Are Fandoms Comparable to Religious Groups?: The Harry Styles Fandom a Case Study', University of Exeter dissertation

Television

'Al Roker/Jenny Slate/Paul Haggis' (2014) Late Night with Seth Meyers.

'Harry Styles/Will Ferrell' (2023) The Late Late Show with James Corden.

'A Goon's Deed in a Weary World' (2013) 30 Rock

Acknowledgements

Right up front, I have to thank Violet Fenn for tagging me in the Facebook post that led to me writing this book and Marc Burrows for the early feedback that made me yelp with joy.

Thank you to Ally and Nora for creating the 1D Slack that led to pretty much everything else.

To Amy for the gifs that changed my world.

To Georgie, Kara, Tanya, Lindsay, Jenni, Ally, Sylvia, Amy, Brigid, Sheena, Andi, Linka, Lucinda, Martina, Kat, Syndea for being the best gig buddies.

To Tabitha Carvan for her hugely entertaining book and our hugely entertaining and enlightening Zoom call.

To the Mollusks for the chicken chat, Dave Grohl thirst, New York brunch. And lizards.

To Alicia, Georgie, Jenni and Kevin for being the GC OGs. I love you all a lot.

To Kat, Syndea, Lucinda and Martina for Australia and, you know, everything else.

And to Ashley, the celebrity dropping by our café. *Finger guns*

To everyone I interviewed for this book and everyone I have talked to about Harry Styles in the past ten years (that will be, I suspect, everyone I've talked to in the past ten years).

To Matt Jabez Alvarez and EmilyPixels for the fabulous photos.

To my agent, Hannah, for not even batting an eye (although we were on the phone, so who knows) when I told her that instead of all the novels I was meant to be writing, I was going to write a book about Harry Styles.

To (my) Harry and Joe for your (mostly) good-natured patience and laughs and love. You're my favourite and my best.

And to Harry Styles. For all the things. But mostly the music. And the face.